Edge of the Anvil

Edge of the Anvil

a resource book for the blacksmith

Text, Illustrations
and Photographs by

Jack Andrews

With a portfolio of photographs of

Samuel Yellin's work

 SkipJack Press
Ocean City, MD

Library of Congress Cataloging in Publication Data

Andrews, Jack
    Edge of the Anvil

    Bibliography: p.
    Includes indes.
    1. Blacksmithing.   I. Title
TT220.A53   682   91-15115

ISBN 1-87953-500-9

Printed in the United States of America

2 4 6 8 10 9 7 5 3 1

Contents

Thanks

I would like to acknowledge and thank the many people that purchased the first book published by Rodale. Thank you for your letters, comments, suggestions and encouragement. It has kept the fires alive and I have truly enjoyed you all as new friends.

A special thanks to Sam Allen, a metallurgist at the Massachusetts Institute of Technology. He has revised and made corrections to the section on Metallurgy. This is the first part of the book to be revised and it is appropriate to have the proper information about the metallurgical aspects of iron clarified.

I would also like to thank the Samuel Yellin Foundation for its continued support of the art and tradition of blacksmithing and their interest and involvement in bringing the new to metalworking. They have also helped me in the support of this work and more.

Since 1985, after the death of Harvey Yellin, I have been working at the Yellin shop. I have shifted from the forge to design work. For the opportunity to specialize in this I would like to thank Marian Yellin and Clare Yellin.

The original concept for this book was that it was a book for the beginner, however there is much knowledge to pass on, so I will be expanding the information in the "Edge of the Anvil" to cover a wider audience. If you have any thoughts about the additions, revisions or corrections please write me at the publisher, SkipJack Press Inc., Box 2460-MBS, Ocean City, MD 21842; or write to my home address, 1482 Maple Avenue, Paoli, PA 19301.

Thank you all!

Introduction and Dedication

"Preserve the old, but know the new." This old Chinese proverb is appropriate as we begin our venture into blacksmithing. We will use what we have learned from the work and writing of masters, and from their techniques and tools and at the same time utilize the best of modern technology and materials. By blending these things we will create new forms.

I have a very strong conviction that there is creative potential and the ability to learn in each of us; everyone is a natural learner who needs only a few guidelines to make his task easier. Therefore I have written this book as if I were giving you instructions; I have tried to anticipate your questions. I have looked back over my own learning experiences at the forge for knowledge to pass on, and have kept in mind the questions that my students at the Philadelphia College of Art have asked during their forging exercises.

I want to emphasize the importance of examining beautiful old pieces and of understanding the processes that were used to make them, because by understanding the techniques that were used by our grandfathers, we can again be craftsmen of iron. Unfortunately, many of the smiths who made these pieces have laid down their hammers, and the techniques have not been passed on to others or recorded in any way. By examining some simple pieces closely, we can see how these old masters worked, and can get a glimpse of the processes that they used to create more complex pieces. This is the reason I have included the photographs of Samuel Yellin's work.

An occasional young blacksmith will have had the opportunity to work with some older smith and to learn from him. Unfortunately, there are only a few old smiths to learn from. So the new smiths have been forced to rediscover the lost techniques and to create new ones. This process of recreating forging techniques is advantageous to today's smiths, for they must follow in the footsteps of their predecessors, who were often self-taught and who had to learn from their mistakes. The smiths of yesteryear gained knowledge, skill and artistry from their search for effective techniques and from their perseverance.

My grandfather started learning about blacksmithing when he was 13. Following this early start, he observed, discovered, and invented methods of working with iron and he formed a business based on his knowledge and skills as a blacksmith. To this sense of discovery and to my grandfather, Charles D. Briddell, Sr., I dedicate this book.

Section I

Blacksmithing

Blacksmithing

The blacksmith of yesteryear brings to mind an image of a robust and independent craftsman who was a main force in the early history of our country. He was a central figure in the life of the village, because he provided most of the tools and implements that were needed for the life of the community. The scale of his work was small, personal and communal.

In some ways, however, he changed this image and brought about his own demise, because he had the knowledge and skills to work iron. He created and invented the tools and processes that were a part of the Industrial Revolution. Most of the early inventors were blacksmiths. The result was a change in life-style from the small shop run by the individual multipurpose craftsman, to the large factory hiring specialized workers for mass production. The result was an abundance of mass-produced goods causing the death of the small-scale operation of the blacksmith. This was true of my grandfather.

Too frequently we have criticized mass production without seeing its benefits. One benefit is that with an abundance of goods, today's craftsmen have been freed to produce those things that have individuality and character.

Perhaps your work with blacksmithing will allow you to reorder your priorities, giving emphasis to new values and providing a new life-style.

Graham Scott Williamson, in his book, *The American Craftsman*, asks, what is craft?

> Where does craft production stop and industrial production begin? . . . Our conception of craft as consisting of the spirit in which, rather than solely the means by which, a production process is carried out. This would appear to be the only conception of craft and craftsmanship which can hope to take root in this technologically advanced age.

Later he quotes Allen Eaton of the Russell Sage Foundation:

> The time will come when every kind of work will be judged by two measurements: one by the product itself, as is now done, and the other by the effect of the work on the producer.

I believe this leads us to some realization that there is hope for the future and that we do not have to be puppets of our culture and technology, but can be forceful in redirecting the thought and movement of our society, if we, as individual craftsmen, set an example by means of our attitudes to our work and towards others.

The ideas set forth and the alternatives suggested in E. F. Schumacher's book, *Small Is Beautiful*, are in striking contrast to the general direction of our country today. Those who read the book may come to feel, as I do, that new attitudes and life-styles are in order.

At a time when there is so much emphasis placed on "progress," growth and expansion on a nationwide scale, it is almost heresy to say, "Small is beautiful." But the two elements can coexist. It is precisely because of the fast pace of all of our lives, the huge industries, vast population and overwhelming bureaucracy, that a reexamination of our values is essential. We see this all around us in the resurgence of interest in crafts of all kinds, in such small things as vegetable gardens and in a return to the "simpler" life. I feel that the village blacksmith's smaller scale of work is the kind of thing with which we should temper today's living. We need not ignore the advances of science and technology, but we must recognize that in the haste to acquire and consume, we ourselves will be consumed.

> The world is too much with us, late and soon.
> Getting and spending, we lay waste our powers. . . .
> W. Wordsworth

Gandhi proposed that we should think in terms of "production by the masses" rather than in terms of "mass production." The home smithy, where only one or two people work, would certainly fall into this category. If work by its nature ennobles and enlightens, then we are working on the development of mind, body and spirit. A technology of "production by the masses" would use the best of modern knowledge and experience to help us to live in ecological balance in the world. It would serve the people; in contrast, in a world devoted to mass production, the people serve the machine. Schumacker calls this "intermediate technology."

The contemporary blacksmith is an example of what is meant by intermediate technology. His work combines the advances of modern technology with the scale of the individual craftsman. He takes pride in each object that he makes and derives pleasure from the creation of beautiful art forms.

> The poetry of the blacksmith shop has been a theme for writers for centuries, but there is little poetry in it to the blacksmith who stands at the forge day after day pounding and shaping unless he has studied, and finds new themes in every heat, spark, or scale. If he can create beautiful forms in his mind, and with his hands shape the metal to those forms, then he can see poetry in his work. If he is but a machine that performs his work automatically, the dull prose of his occupation makes him dissatisfied and unmanly. [M. T. Richardson; *Practical Blacksmithing*, vol. III]

How do you see your forging, as poetry or work? It is vital to see it as poetry, if you wish to find satisfaction.

Even poetry must be structured, and before you can make anything at the forge, you must design it. There are many factors that influence the design process. Some of these are: personal direction and attitude, experience and observation, historical perspective, current trends, the function of the piece and its placement, and finally the material and the forming processes used to create it. Your work will be influenced more strongly by certain factors than by others; this is what makes artistic creation individualized. No one way is the "right" way.

Don't be intimidated into thinking that you can't design. You can. Do it, and you will find that each time you work, you will improve, because the experience of forging and the work itself will give you feedback. Be your own most severe critic, but at the same time, talk to others about your work.

A powerful design influence on your work is your own personal direction, life-style and attitude. Your work will express your own personality and creativity; it will be you.

Your experience will be a major influence. Your design will reflect your travel and studies.

Historical perspective affects your design considerably. As you become familiar with the rich heritage of blacksmithing and learn about the development of ironwork, you will be inspired. When you study different periods in the development of iron, you will gain a greater understanding of the forms and the reasons for their design. It is interesting to copy one of your favorite old pieces, first making it the way it was originally made, and then making another one, this time using your ideas and methods.

History is being made by the new generation of smiths. They will soon be influential, because their work has the power to excite your imagination, and lead you to new ideas of your own. Study their work. The entire contemporary culture, for that matter, can give you inspiration.

The most powerful factors affecting design will be the material itself, the tools used and the processes involved in forming it. Forging iron is a direct working process. You will see this direct quality in the photographs of Yellin's work in section V.

It is exciting to try to combine another material, such as wood, clay, leather, glass, plastic or fiber, with iron, as a challenging exercise in design. Explore the relationship of iron and the other material, using the two substances in different ways together.

Because the forging process itself and the tools that you use have such a powerful form-giving potential, you might want to create a process or design a new tool. This would in turn be a design influence. If you are making many similar or identical pieces, the design of the tools used to make them influences the design of the pieces themselves.

The formal aspects of design, such as control of line, plane, shape, space and texture, are important. If you have training, then it can be used to good advantage; if not, art courses will give you the formal knowledge that will enable you to design and analyze your work. But don't feel that you can't design because you have not been to art school. You can, and you do it everyday in all areas of your life, by dealing with other problems or challenges creatively and imaginatively. Incorporate this habit into your work with iron.

I do my designing in my sketchbook, which is nothing more than an

8 x 10 bound, plain paper book. If I have an idea for a new piece of iron or a new way to work it, I draw it here. I really enjoy this book, because it is the place where I can give form to my ideas and have fun with them. First, I envision the complete piece and then I draw it to understand how it will be forged. This process has been invaluable to me, because many of my trials and errors have been on paper and not at the forge. This has saved me a lot of time.

A work session at the drawing board is as important as a work session at the forge. This is as true today as it was at the turn of the century, when the following was written:

> The young man who thinks of learning the blacksmith trade should first learn whether he is physically fitted for the peculiar labor. If satisfied on that point, he should immediately begin a course of study with special reference to the working of metals. He should also study freehand drawing. Every hour spent at the drawing board is an hour spent shaping irons, as he is training the hand to perform the work and the eye to see that it is true. And at no time should he drop the pencil. He should keep in mind the fact that the most skillful are the most successful. We do not mean skillful in one line only, but in all. The man who can direct, as well as execute, is the one who will make the greatest advancement, and to direct it is necessary to know why a thing should be done as well as how. [M. T. Richardson, *Practical Blacksmithing*, vol. III]

Drawing is a tool as essential to the blacksmith as the hammer. Drawing gives form to ideas, just as the hammer gives form to the metal. If you try to forge without preparation, forging will be more difficult. You may occasionally want to experiment at the forge, but in general, it is a good idea to plan your work ahead of time. Try working for a whole day at the forge without any preparation and see what happens.

There is one very important aspect of drawing that I want to stress: Anyone can draw, but it takes practice and experience to draw well. So start; the more that you draw, the better your drawings will be.

There is a way to draw three-dimensionally, and that is by using clay as a sketch medium. You can give substance to your ideas by forming in clay those things that you would like to form later in iron at the forge. Clay is a good medium in which to practice while you are assembling your equipment and setting up your forge. You will undoubtedly create many new forms and perhaps invent a new tool or a new technique.

Not only can you sketch with clay, but also you can use it in place of iron to practice the forging operations before lighting up. Clay, like hot iron, is plastic and can be easily formed. But hot iron cannot be directly felt and worked with your hands; it must be worked quickly and with tools. In contrast, clay can be worked with your hands at leisure. Practice some of the first forging exercises in clay, and then design a few pieces to make at the forge.

Who is the piece for and where does it go? These questions will challenge you to come up with some original creations. If you are just forging things for yourself and your own enjoyment, then the design of your work will be different than it would be if you are selling your work. My cousin, Don Briddell, who is a maker of painted wildfowl carvings, said it very well:

> I've found an important ingredient is respect for the customer. Too many creators value their way too much. To make a customer happy is as much a part of the design as any other element. Ask yourself: "Am I in this to make myself happy or the customer?" The best solution is to arrive at a design that makes both of you happy. Arrogance does in many an artist, as does its inverse, submissiveness. A good designer finds the middle way in these matters. Let it be known that such a design exists.

I think you should focus your thinking on what you are going to do with your blacksmithing. The focus of your blacksmithing work can take many forms: You can be anything from a full-time smith to just an interested person. Only you can determine the scope of your involvement and commitment to blacksmithing. If your approach is casual and leisurely, you will not need to be too organized. However, if you intend to devote a lot of time to blacksmithing, or if you are considering earning part or even all of your livelihood from smithing, then make plans and get organized! I recommend *The Craftsman's Survival Manual* by George and Nancy Wettlaufer and *How to Organize and Operate a Small Business* by C. M. Baumbeck, K. Lawyer, and P. C. Kelly.

Blacksmithing

If you are one of those who intends to start your own business, then you should plan to develop your image, your selling strategy and business procedures.

Your reputation as a person and as a craftsman is the most important factor involved in selling your work. If you excell, you can count on word-of-mouth advertising.

A good portfolio will do a good selling job for you, too. Photograph your work as you do it. I wish I had done this, because I have already forgotten some of my early pieces.

A well-designed business card and stationery are also helpful in creating an image, selling your work and meeting the public. Eventually you might want to tag each piece to explain it and compile a catalogue. Keep all of these visually coordinated. The result will be an image of yourself that will come across to the public: a blending of your work, personality and the above visual aids. Work on your image and forge it as well as you forge your iron.

Records are an important part of running a business. The "job-work file" is the most important of your records. This is the record of each job and contains the vital information about it, including billing. Mine is made up on 5 x 8 cards. I use a work card for every job. I number them consecutively, and file them when the job is completed. These cards form the basis for my work schedule.

Start and continue your blacksmithing in an orderly way.

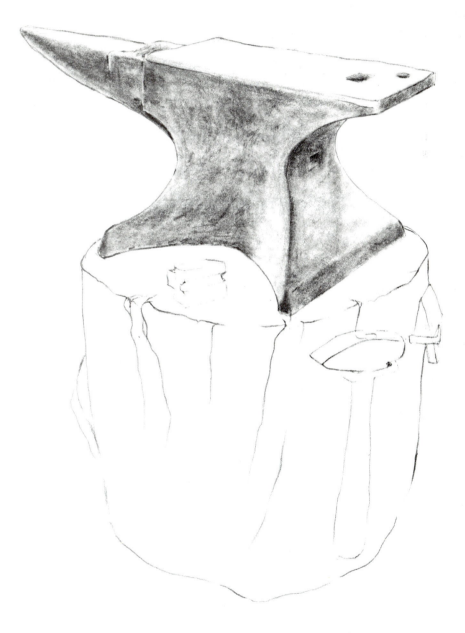

Section II

Tools and Equipment

Your first look around a smithy might be confusing because of the great variety of unfamiliar tools and equipment covered with dust, their seeming disarray and the poor light. However, an experienced smith looks in on an order and working arrangement with the light of knowledge. This section is organized to bring that order and light as you begin your study of blacksmithing.

The Smithy

The smithy is the building in which the blacksmith does his work. This term is frequently confused with another, the smith, who is the person doing the blacksmithing. Don't, however, confuse the space in which the smith works with the way he feels about it. Good working relationships and attitudes must exist for good work to be done.

My first smithy was a shed with one side open. It was an interesting starting point, but I allowed junk to clutter the working space and soon things were disorganized. I soon realized that this had an adverse effect on the way I worked. I was easily discouraged. I began to plan and think about the different types of buildings I could construct. After a long search, I discovered what I was looking for: the tipi. One is now set up in the woods behind my home. My sons and I cut the poles in the woods and I ordered the cover from California. The tipi is 20 feet in diameter. The sun filters through the canvas, providing good working light all day. By adjusting the smoke flaps, I can control the ventilation. On stormy days, when there is a strong southerly wind, I don't work, I watch the woods in-

stead. The tipi was not expensive, it was easy to erect, and it is portable.

The tipi has another quality which is important to me (aside from being true American architecture). That is the quality of the workspace. It is a truly enjoyable place to work and I like being there. The tipi is quiet (sounds do not reverberate).

I have concluded that there is no ideal smithy. Construct one to suit yourself.

The primary consideration when building a smithy should be adequate space. Set aside an area, as you begin to collect your equipment and arrange it. (You can work outside, but this should only be a temporary arrangement.) Now consider the ways in which various pieces of equipment interact. Things may be convenient and orderly, but unless they relate in a functional manner, it will be difficult to work.

Working Relationships

The diagram shows the interrelationships of the pieces of equipment. They are not drawn to scale. The amount of time spent at each location is indicated by the size of the circles and arrows. You can now see the relative value of each piece of equipment. The general working relationships are illustrated here. This diagram can serve as a guideline for setting up your own equipment. (Since I am righthanded, the diagram is set up for those working right-handed; southpaws can reverse the diagram here, and at other places in the book.)

Most of your work will be done between the forge and the anvil. Therefore, each step that you save and each turn that you can shorten

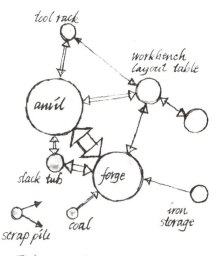

Diagram of working relationships

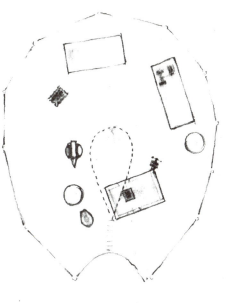

Layout in tipi

13

will be to your advantage. You may want to vary the distance from the forge to the anvil depending on the kind of work that you are doing. They can be close together when you are doing small pieces, but you will need more space when you are doing large pieces. Set up your forge and anvil first, and then arrange the other things around them. The workbench, layout table, tool rack and other items can easily be moved.

I rake the earthen floor in my tipi everyday before I start work. At the end of the day, I can see my footprints and my work pattern. The diagram was developed from this pattern. After working in the tipi for a while, I found that some of my right-angled arrangements were not very good. So, I made some changes.

When you are visiting another smith and watching him work, try to see how he uses his space and try to imagine how this would work for you. Watching the hot metal is fun, but don't ignore the steps that he takes, his stance and posture, and the way in which he uses the tools and the space around him.

I assume throughout this book that you will be working by yourself while you are learning forging. This means that you will be a single-handed smith. The descriptions and exercises are selected with this in mind. Later, some of the exercises will call for a striker or a hammer man. You will then need more space and a slightly different arrangement for your equipment, because the striker stands on the side of the anvil opposite the smith.

The other important features of a good smithy are: Proper light, good ventilation, safety and order.

Light

It should be fairly obvious that you need enough light to see the work that you are doing, but many smiths ignore this important consideration. Working in direct sunlight can be a problem. It is difficult to see the color of the hot metal and to ascertain the temperature.

> If smiths would go to work and wash their windows, clean out behind their bellows, pick up the scrap that lies promiscuously about the shop, gather up the bolts, etc., they would be surprised at the change that it would make, not only in the general appearance of their shop, but also in the ease and convenience of doing work. One great disadvantage under which most smiths labor is the lack of light. Frequently blacksmith shops are stuck down in a basement or in some remote corner of a building. It is a fact, whether it be disregarded or not, that it is easier to do good work in a clean, well-lighted shop than in one which is dirty and dark. [M. T. Richardson, *Practical Blacksmithing*, vol. I, p. 75]

Ventilation

Good ventilation is vital for your health. You must have a chimney and hood that draw properly. It will draw out the smoke and will help keep the ash from flying around. In addition, it will help to maintain the fire when you are away.

There are two types of chimneys: one made of brick, and the other of sheet metal and smoke pipe. Unless you are an experienced mason or smith, it is best to plan something simple. The hood may either be attached to or hung over the forge, depending on your preference, although the bell hood will not draw as well. Think about the ways in which the chimney will be affected by things outside it, such as the shape of the roof, trees and prevailing winds.

When you are setting up your forge, think about the flow of fresh air through the smithy. It is important that windows and doors be positioned to allow an even flow of cool air into the smithy.

Another important feature of the smithy is the floor. I have worked on concrete floors, but they are hard on the feet and legs. In addition, it is difficult to "set" your anvil and other equipment on a concrete floor. The dirt floor in my tipi is better. Holmstrom says:

> A plank floor is a great nuisance around the anvil. Every piece cut off hot is to be hunted up and picked up or it will set fire to it. I know there will be some objection to this kind of floor, but if you once learn how to keep it you will change your mind. To make this floor take sand and clay with fine gravel, mix with coal dust and place a layer where wanted about four inches thick. This floor, when a little old, will be as hard as iron, provided you sprinkle it every night with water. The dust and soot from the shop will, in time, settle in with it and it will be smooth and hard. It will not catch fire; no cracks for small tools or bolts to fall through; it will not crack like cement or brick floors. [J. G. Holmstrom, *Modern Blacksmithing*, p. 31]

The Anvil

The anvil is the king of the tools for the blacksmith. Its design has been developed over the centuries. New anvils are expensive and hard to find. Look around for a used one. (Unfortunately, collectors and antique dealers are looking, too.)

There are several important things to look for when you are buying an anvil: the size, weight and general condition. Listen to the ring of the anvil when it is struck. Cran says:

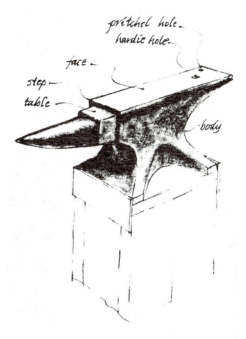

> The quality of an anvil can generally be judged by its "ring," a good anvil giving out a sharp, clear sound when struck with a hammer; if soft or not free from flaws, the sound will be dull. A good anvil mounted on a block in such a manner that it gives out its full volume of sound is easier to work upon than one where the ring is deadened. [James Cran, *Machine Blacksmithing*, p. 23]

Hit the anvil lightly and notice how the hammer responds. Does it jump back up or does it just lie there? The hammer is partially lifted by the life of the anvil. A lively anvil will make your work much easier. A forged anvil will respond well; in contrast, cast-iron anvils have a tendency to be dead and full.

The main working parts of the anvil are the horn, the face and the edge; if these are not in good shape, you will have problems. Examine the horn for excessive chisel marks or dents; if it is only lightly marred, it can be filed. Check the face for sinks; if they are not too deep, you can work around them. If there are large, long chips on the outer edge, consider passing up the anvil. If you are a good arc welder, you

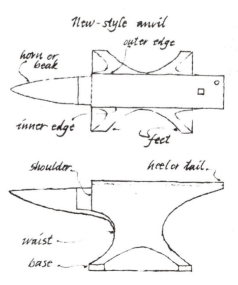

17

will be able to fill the chips and sinks and regrind the face.

Any used anvil will be worn in areas. This is not always bad. My anvil, an older style of unknown origin, has a shallow but smoothly worn area on the face about one fourth of the way from the step. This slight depression is an advantage when I am straightening and bending, and most of the time, it is out of the way, since I prefer to do most of my work about one third to one half the distance from the step.

In general, you will need an anvil that weighs somewhere between 100 and 140 pounds, depending on the type of work that you will be doing. When you are working single-handed and doing light work, a small anvil will be sufficient, but when you are working with a striker, you will need a heavier anvil. In general, it is better to have a heavier anvil than a lighter one. The weight of the anvil is described by the numbers on the side. It is a very old system based on the hundredweight, which is equal to 112 pounds. The first number is in full hundredweight, the second number is in quarters of hundredweight, and the third is in actual pounds. An anvil marked 112 is the sum of 112, 28 and 2, or 142 pounds. The new-style anvils have their weight marked in pounds.

The top view shows the edges of a typical anvil; the cross section shows the way in which the edges should be ground. The edge from a to b is the portion that is used most often. The edge from a to b should be ground to ⅜-inch radius. Blend it into a ¼-inch radius from b to c. Grind the edge from d to e to ¼-inch radius. The edge of the heel can be

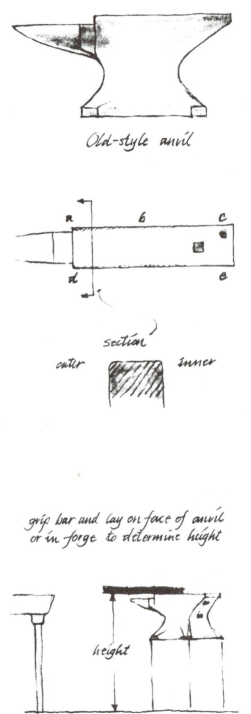

Old-style anvil

section

outer   inner

grip bar and lay on face of anvil
or in forge to determine height

height

either sharp or rounded. Some anvils have never had their edges dressed in this manner; as a result, they will be excessively chipped.

Sometimes a smith will leave a sharp edge on the anvil. He will use the sharp edge of the heel to cut stock, instead of using the hardie. Be careful when you do this; it is potentially dangerous, because pieces of metal can easily be chipped from the hammer or the edge of the anvil.

Setting the Anvil

"Setting the anvil" means placing it in position. It is absolutely vital to have the anvil on a stand, at the right height and distance from the forge. You will probably go through a bit of jockeying around to find the proper position, but once this has been established, it is best to anchor the stand or sink it in the floor. In general, you should be able to hold a piece of iron comfortably on the face of the anvil.

You can make the stand for the anvil from a log of elm or oak. Sink the log into the ground a foot or more. This anchors it securely. Make sure that the anvil is held firmly to the stand and that it does not slip or slide. You can secure it with heavy spikes.

The Forge

The forge is an open hearth where the smith makes his fire. It is made up of: the tuyere and firebox, a hood or chimney, the hearth, and the blower or bellows. Small portable forges are usually found on farms. The Champion 400 is larger and good for general smithing.

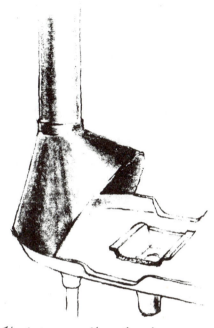

Hood for 400 Champion forge

Chimney forge

Tools and Equipment

The forge that I made to use in the tipi is built of 4 × 4 oak lumber, with a new Buffalo firebox and tuyere, an old blower and a steel plate holding the hearth (which is firebrick and General Refactories fireclay). I have bolted a post vise to the lefthand corner. This is an extremely handy arrangement, because it provides space for a large working area around the vise. There is also a small surface plate at the corner; this doubles as a small anvil. It is convenient to have racks on the sides of the forge to hold tongs and other tools. Sometimes a coal bin and a water trough are built into the forge. Most smiths use a slack tub, which is a large container of water, placed close to the forge and anvil. A coal bucket is also handy.

Champion 400

If the anvil is king, then the forge is the alchemist, for the forge contains the transforming fire. The fire transforms the metal into a plastic medium, making it easy to work and form. The fire also changes the crystalline structure of the metal, causing changes in its physical properties.

Portable forge

Tuyere

Tuyere is a French term derived from the word *tuyau*, meaning blowpipe. Through it, the blast of air enters the forge, and creates the intense heat needed for forging. It controls the size and character of the fire by its shape and the amount of air allowed to the fire. The type of tuyere that is commonly used today was preceded by the side-blast tuyere. The side-blast tuyere had to be water-cooled to keep from burning and clogging with clinkers.

The simplest of all tuyeres is a pipe with a

tipi forge

hole in the middle. One end is plugged, the other attached to the blower. It is installed so the fire will be built over the hole.

The firebox is made of fireclay and brick. This is serviceable and will get you started, although there is no grate or ash dump.

The following chart will act as a guideline in determining sizes for the forge and tuyere:

Side-blast tuyere

Tuyere opening	¾"	1"	1⅜"
Depth of firebox	4"	5"	6"
Diameter of supply pipe	1¾"	2"	2½"
Size of work	¼-1"	1-2"	2-4"

The air pressure should be at least 8 ounces per square inch.

Place the hood close to the hearth to catch the smoke. Don't forget, if it is too high, it loses drawing power; if it is too large, it can get in the way of your work. The hood should be vented as directly as possible.

A blast of air, generated either by means of a bellows or a mechanical blower, will provide the oxygen that the fire needs, and will bring the fire to a high temperature. Most smiths use a blower. It is important to be able to control the amount of air; this can be done with a rheostat on the motor or a butterfly valve in the blast tube. The control for the air blast should be easy to reach, since you will cut the blast each time iron is taken from the fire. Usually the blower is mounted on a shelf underneath the forge. It will then be out of the way, but close to the tuyere. (Even an old vacuum cleaner can be used.)

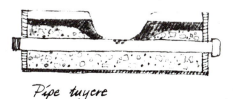

Pipe tuyere

Workbench

You will be doing many different things at the workbench. It is important to have several things at hand: a bench grinder for dressing tools, a wire brush for cleaning and finishing, and a vise and related hand tools for finishing operations. Be sure that you have enough space to lay out drawings and complex parts for assembly.

There are many other tools that you will find handy: an assortment of files, a hacksaw, drills, a drill press, a band saw and many others that you might already have. The main thing is: Consider the organization of these tools and the way in which they are used and stored, in much the same way that you consider the arrangement of the forge and anvil.

The Hammer

"By the hammer and the hand all the arts do stand." The hammer is the prince of the blacksmith's tools. In the pursuit of any other craft using materials that can be handled, such as clay, wood, leather or fiber, the craftsman feels the material. The hammer is of vital importance to the smith, because in blacksmithing, the smith gets the feel of the iron through the hammer.

The distinguishing characteristics of a hammer are the part called the peen, which is the end of the head opposite the face, and the weight of the hammer. It is the shape of the peen which enables us to differentiate between different types of hammers. In general, a hammer that weighs between 2 and 3 pounds will be adequate, although you may occasionally need something lighter or heavier.

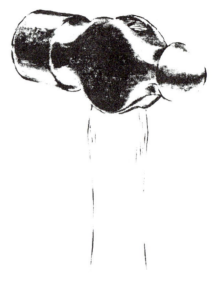

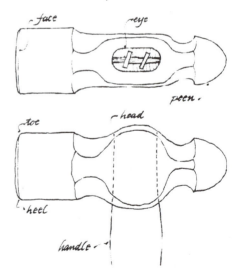

Ball peen hammer

The head of the hammer is made of tool steel which has been heat-treated. The face and peen are hard and durable; in contrast, the body is tough, strong and resiliant. When you are buying a new hammer, redress the face, so that it will not mar the iron. The eye of the hammer holds the handle. Note the difference between the top of the eye and the bottom of the eye. The large wooden wedge expands the top of the handle to the sides and the small steel wedges tighten it securely.

Hammer handles are usually made of hickory because of its strength, long clean grain and resiliancy, but sometimes ash is substituted. The handle must be securely attached and aligned at a right angle to the head. A faulty alignment can result in misdirected blows. The shape is fullest about two-thirds of the way down the handle, making this the most comfortable place to grip the handle. It is best to treat the handle with linseed oil; the wood will then ensure a firm grip. Never varnish, lacquer, or shellac the handle, for if you do, your hand will slip.

cross peen

straight peen

factory face   redressed

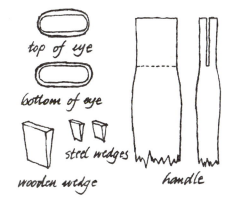

top of eye

bottom of eye

steel wedges

wooden wedge   handle

23

Sledges

Sledges are heavier than hammers, and are used by the striker. The hand sledges (sometimes called the uphand sledge) weigh between 5 and 10 pounds. The swing sledges are heavier, up to 20 pounds, with longer handles. The striker does not raise the hand sledge over his head, but the swing sledge he swings like an ax. The striker must be skillful to use the swing sledge effectively and safely.

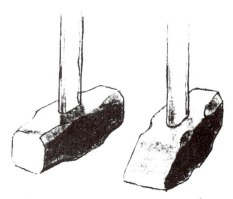

Double-faced   Cross-peen sledges

Tongs

Plan your work so that the iron can be held in your hand. However, you will find as the work progresses that eventually you must cut off the piece and hold it with tongs. You will also find that you will need more tongs than of any other tool. Consider making an open tong rack. You should be able to see and reach the tongs easily.

Tongs are referred to by the task that they do or by the shape of the jaws or bits. For example, pickup tongs are used at the forge for picking up pieces in the fire, and are not used for holding iron while forging.

The handles are called reins. If you slide a ring, or coupler, on the end of the reins and force it on tightly, you can grip the iron securely with the jaws of the tongs. This will allow you to manipulate the tongs easily while maintaining a secure grip on the iron. You will need rings in several sizes.

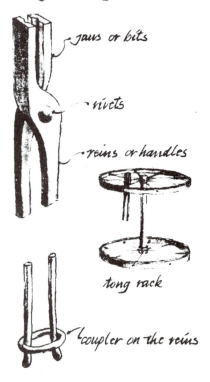

Flat-jawed tongs

jaws or bits

rivets

reins or handles

tong rack

coupler on the reins

Vises

The vise is the third hand of the smith. There are two types of vises, the machinist vise, and the post, box or stake vise. The machinist vise, or bench vise, is the most familiar; it is used to hold or clamp the metal when you are finishing a project or doing light work. Its jaws remain parallel during its entire operation. The post vise hinges and the jaws do not remain parallel; this is because the jaws are hinged. Both of the jaws are joined to the post; when a blow is struck, the force travels down the post into its foundation. The screw-thread assembly does not receive any of the force and will not break as it might on a machinist vise. Mount the post vise securely on a heavy bench with a good base, which will absorb the force of the blows.

When you are looking at old post vises, look at the screw assembly. Examine the screw and hemispherical washer for excessive wear. If the spring that holds the jaws open is missing, a new one can be made. A new holding or mounting plate can also be made, if necessary.

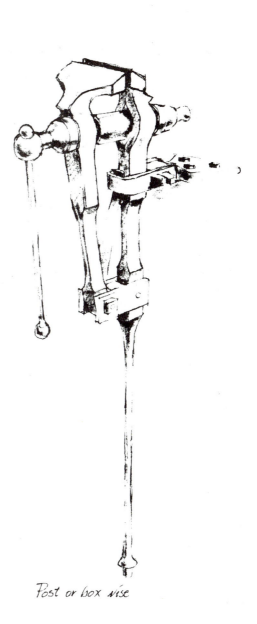

Post or box vise

Anvil Tools

The anvil tools, that is, tools which are used in the anvil, make up the court of the king.

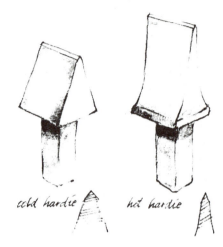

cold hardie   hot hardie

Hardies

The hardie is the anvil tool that is used most often. In use, they are placed in the square hole in the anvil, which is known as the hardie hole. Hardies are used to cut hot or cold metal. Iron can be cut off flush with the cutoff hardies.

The hardie is a bottom tool. It has a mate which does the same job, but which is held on the top of the piece. The hardie's mate is a chisel. This is the top tool. The top tool may or may not have a handle. The ones with handles are called either hot or cold sets (or sate). They are always struck with a sledge, and are never swung like a hammer. When you use a tool with a handle, you will not burn yourself, and you will be less likely to strike your hand with the sledge.

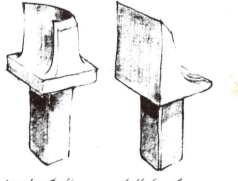

round cut-off   cut-off hardie

Top and bottom tools can be used singly or as matched pairs. When top and bottom tools are used together, they cut iron easily.

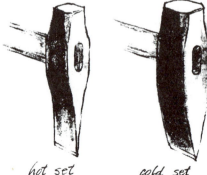

hot set   cold set

Fullers

The top and bottom fullers are used to spread metal in a horizontal direction, in other words, to reduce the cross section. They are basic forming tools that act just like your fingers when you are squeezing clay. Used together or singly, they start many forming operations in forging. The spreading fuller is used to spread, as well as to make right-angle bends.

Swages

Swages are forming tools used to shape and finish the iron. You can make swages to create any desired cross section of metal. The spring swage is a good example. The spring swage is useful to the single-handed smith, for he can hold the iron and strike the top part of the swage at the same time.

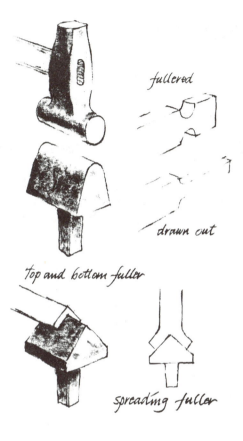

fullered

drawn out

Top and bottom fuller

spreading fuller

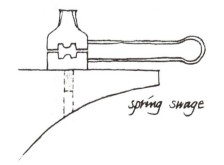

spring swage

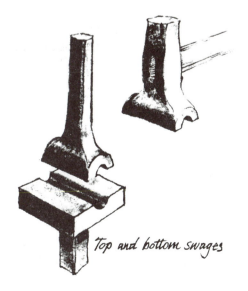

Top and bottom swages

Tools and Equipment

Swage Block

The swage block is a multi-use bottom tool that is sometimes called a swage anvil. It can be used in two positions: lying down or standing up on its edge. Use the holes for heading, bending, shaping and forming.

Flatter

The flatter, or flattie, is the tool used to smooth out the surface of the metal when there are hammer marks and other imperfections.

Set Hammer

The set hammer is slightly smaller than the flattie. It has a sharper edge to get into corners, shoulders and other areas the flattie could not reach. It is used like a hammer, but because the hammer cannot always be controlled in tight areas, the set hammer is used instead.

Set hammer

Punches

Punches are used to punch holes. Round, square and oval punches are the most common. You can make other shapes as needed. A bolster is the base placed under the iron when you are punching a hole. The punch will go through the iron and through the hole in the bolster.

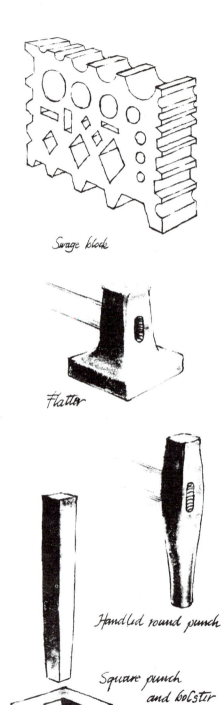

Swage block

Flatter

Handled round punch

Square punch and bolster

Mandril

Mandrils are used to form circular shapes and rings. The smaller mandril fits into the hardie hole. The larger mandril weighs 100 pounds or more and stands on the floor. When the small mandril is bent over, it is called an anvil beak, because it is a smaller version of the beak on the anvil. It may even be shaped like a small anvil.

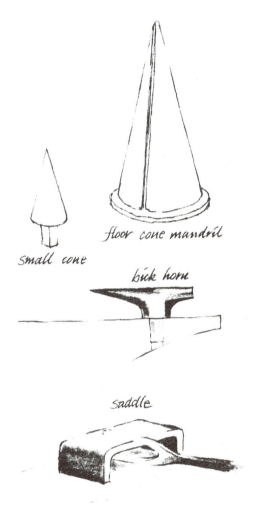

floor cone mandril

small cone

bick horn

Cupping Tool

The cupping tool is a finishing tool used to clean up the head of a rivet. The companion to the cupping tool is the rivet set, which is placed on the bottom side of the rivet being formed, so that it will not be flattened.

saddle

rivet set *and cupping tool*

Saddle

A saddle is used to form the jaws of open-ended wrenches and the tines on forks, when the horn of the anvil is unsuitable.

Heading Tool

A heading tool is used to make heads on nails and bolts. It is a piece of metal with one or more tapered holes in it.

heading tool

Tools and Equipment

Nail Header

The nail header has a raised face. This makes it easy to finish the head of the nail with angled blows.

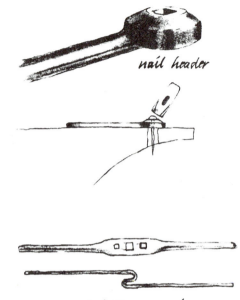

nail header

Twisting Wrenches

Twisting wrenches provide the balance and leverage for twisting heavy sections of iron. You can use small adjustable pliers, pipe wrenches or Vise Grips to twist small pieces of metal, but since they have only one handle, the twisting action is not balanced. This can cause a wobble in the twist.

twisting wrenches

bending fork and bending wrench

Drifts

A drift is used to open or form a hole. The most common are oval-shaped ones, which are used to develop the eye for a hammer. Leave them in place while you are forming the hammer head.

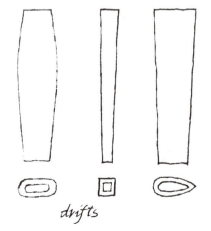

drifts

Cutting Saddle

The cutting saddle, or cutting plate, is used to split or cut iron when the piece is too large for the step of the anvil.

Cutoff Tools

The cutoff tools are used to shear off iron. They are useful when you are cutting off a number of similar pieces of iron, for example, when you are making chain links.

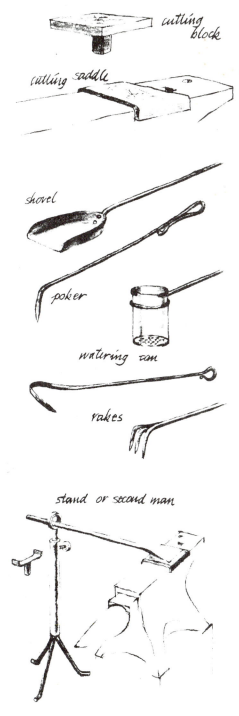

Fire Tools

Tools used at the forge are called either fire or forge tools. The most common are the poker, rake, shovel and watering can. Stands and supports are used at the anvil and the forge to hold the work, leaving the tong hand free. They are sometimes called the "second man" or the "blacksmith's helper."

Measuring Tools

Use standard measuring tools at the forge. They should be made of metal so they will not be burned. The hook rule is handy. You can measure hot iron easily by hooking the tip over the end of the iron. Use chalk or a soapstone pencil for general marking, but when you want to mark a piece that will be placed in the fire, use a center punch. Calipers are used to check the thickness of iron as it is being forged. Travelers are used to measure rounds or irregular lines. They are about 3 inches in diameter and have a circumference of about 1 foot. To measure a piece, roll the traveler along the piece and count the revolutions.

hook rule

calipers   *dividers*

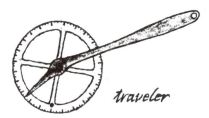

traveler

Safety

Your eyes should be protected. I highly recommend that you wear safety glasses. Hot scale and chips of steel can severely burn and damage your eyes. Radiation from a welding fire is a hazard, too.

Do not wear synthetic clothing while you are working, since it catches fire quickly. Cotton clothing is better. Wear a cotton or leather apron to protect yourself against some of the heat and dirt. Some smiths wear only a half apron.

Wear a leather glove on your tong hand when you are holding warm metal and tools. But avoid using a glove on your hammer hand, since you will lose control and the feel of the metal. Harden your hand with work. A word of caution: If you are used to wearing gloves when picking up hot metal, you may forget and do the same thing when you don't have gloves on and you will be burned.

The last time I wore low-cut shoes in the forge, a hot slug from a punched hole dropped into my shoe. I thought it was a bee at first. I recommend that your shoes come up under your pants to protect you and provide good support.

Coal

The production of coal takes many eons of time. The process begins with the growth of plants, which become peat; this in turn is gradually compressed into coal. It is estimated that it takes three feet of peat to make a seam of bituminous coal one foot thick. Under the proper conditions, the peat goes through the following stages as it is transformed into coal: peat, brown coal, lignite, sub-bituminous, bituminous, semi-anthracite and anthracite.

We are concerned only with bituminous coal. A dry analysis of bituminous coal would range as follows:

Ash	7-11 percent
Fixed carbon	60-78 percent
Volatile matter	11-33 percent

By looking at this analysis, you can see that only 7 to 11 percent of the material will not burn; this part will form the ash and clinker. Coke is the desired fuel for the smith; to obtain this, you drive off the volatile matter and burn it. This process is called coking, and it is done at every work session at the forge. The coke made at the forge is called breeze, since it is light and easily broken apart. (In contrast, metallurgical coke is heavier and difficult to break apart. It is made basically for the steel industry, but is useful when you are welding. It is also difficult to light and not as easy to use in the forge, because it is so hard.)

You can easily break blacksmithing coal apart in your hands. Examine it for white flakes or brown and yellow spots; these are impurities and sulfur. The pieces of coal should be no larger than a dime and contain about 20- to 30-percent fines. Fines is the coal dust and is important in cementing the mass of coal together as coke. (You may have noticed by now the linquistic shorthand that the blacksmith uses: "flattie," "heading tool," "breeze," and "fines." These terms are direct and delightfully simple.) To summarize, your coal should have little ash, be high-bituminous, be the correct size, be free from sulfur and have the right amount of fines mixed with it.

You can check the coal when it is burning by examining the color of the flame; it should be a bright, clean, light orange glow. The bed of the fire should be a uniform color without hot spots. If the fire has hot spots and "drops out," that is, burns out rapidly, then the coal is questionable for forging. Examine the coke around the edges of the fire; it should be solid and be a clear, dark grey color. If it is not, it is dirty.

Anthracite coal is used only for special operations at the forge. It is difficult to light, but is almost pure carbon. It gives off a great deal of heat and lasts a long time, so it is used where high temperatures and a clean fire are needed.

Charcoal was the first fuel used by smiths. It is sometimes used today when a lower temperature and a clean fire are desired. It is lighter than coal and can easily be blown out of the firebox with the blast. Charcoal is used when working with high carbon steels to prevent them from being decarburized.

Gas and electricity are used in industry for various types of forging and heat-treating operations, but are not ordinarily used by the independent smith.

Iron

Iron is the black metal and the blacksmith is so named because that is the metal that he works, not because he usually gets so dirty while working at the forge. When a piece of iron is placed in the fire, it rapidly oxidizes, forming a layer of black scale. At an orange heat (1,740°F.) the scale will readily fall off, but at a light cherry (1,550°F.), the scale adheres and the iron remains black. You can remove the scale by chemical and mechanical means, but you may not want to, because this color is one of the positive attributes of the iron. You can enhance it with various finishes.

A "heat" refers to each time that a piece of iron is heated. The scale formed during each heat amounts to about 1 percent of the total weight of the iron. It is easy to see that you can lose much of your iron if you use an excessive number of heats. A good smith will always do the work required in as few heats as possible.

Iron in its natural state is in the form of iron oxides. Pig iron is the iron that is extracted by means of a pyrochemical process in the blast furnace. Other iron products, such as wrought iron, cast iron and steel, are made from pig iron. For a good understanding of these processes, read *The Making, Shaping and Treating of Steel*, by U. S. Steel.

Cast Iron

Cast iron is made by mixing pig iron with other grades of iron and steel, depending upon its future use. Cast iron is not a material that can be forged, yet many things in the smithy are made of cast iron.

Wrought Iron

Wrought iron is best described as a two-component metal consisting of high-purity iron and iron silicate—a particular type of glass-like slag. The iron and the slag are in physical association, as contrasted to the chemical or alloy relationship that generally exists between the constituents of other metals. Wrought iron is the only ferrous metal that contains siliceous slag. [*Wrought Iron and Its Manufacture, Characteristics, and Applications*, James Aston and Edward B. Story]

Wrought iron is so called because during the process of its manufacture, it is worked with large hammers to combine the slag with the iron. The amount of siliceous slag in wrought iron varies from 1 to 3 percent by weight. This slag gives wrought iron its fibrous character. You can easily determine whether a piece is wrought iron by nicking it with a cold chisel and bending it. There will be fibers (like the ones in wood) in the wrought iron, rather than grains, which you would find in steel. Wrought iron is resistant to corrosion because of the purity of the iron and because of the slag.

It is easier to forge and weld wrought iron than any of the other iron metals. It is worked at a yellow heat (2,100–2,200°F.) and welded at a white heat (2,500°F.).

Although wrought iron is still made in Europe, unfortunately it is no longer made in the United States. You will be lucky if you can find someone who has a supply of it (this is most unlikely); otherwise you will have to scout around for it at a scrapyard, or when old buildings are demolished.

Steel

Steel is a combination of iron and carbon; it also will always contain manganese, phosphorus, sulfur and silicon. There is a long list of other alloys that can greatly vary the properties of the steel. Carbon, however, is the major alloy of iron. The amount of carbon in the steel will range from a trace to about 1.70 percent. In the language of the blacksmith, this would be 170 points of carbon. Thus a point is 0.01 percent. A 1-percent carbon steel would have 100 points of carbon, and a 0.45-percent steel would have 45 points. Steels are graded by the amount of carbon they contain.

Mild or low carbon steel	1-40	points
High carbon steel	40-60	points
Spring steel	70-80	points
Tool steel	80-170	points

Alloy steels are steels that contain elements other than carbon as their major alloying elements. They have enhanced physical properties as the result of these alloys. There is a more complete discussion of iron and steel in the sections "Metallurgy for the Blacksmith" and "Identification of Metals."

Hereafter, in order to make things simple, the generic name of *iron* will be used when the various techniques and processes are described. When a specific alloy is required for a task or tool, then the specific name will be used.

Getting Started

If you had all of the tools just surveyed, your forge would be very well equipped, but you can get started with just a few. (An excellent book to help you understand more about your search for tools is H. R. Bradley Smith's book *Blacksmith and Farriers' Tools at the Shelburne Museum*.)

First of all, establish where you will be working and begin to plan the space. As you gather tools and the equipment, place them and check out the working relationships. Plan for the forge immediately as it will be the largest piece of equipment and most difficult to set. Work out the ventilation and light. When you place the anvil and set it on its stand, do it properly, to avoid the frustration of having it slide around. Now plan for other large pieces of equipment, if you have them.

You will need several hammers to begin with. I suggest a ball peen weighing around 2 pounds and a cross peen that is slightly heavier, up to 3 pounds. A couple of pairs of tongs (to grip ¼- to ½-inch stock) will be helpful in the beginning; you can add more later. Vise Grips and pliers will fill in the gaps initially. A hardie or a cold chisel is a must.

Good coal is absolutely necessary, as are a bucket and shovel for the coal, and a slack tub nearby. Visit the steel scrapyards and scrounge the countryside for steel. To start, try to get ¼-inch, ⅜-inch and ½-inch rounds and squares, and then stockpile other sizes. Axles, coil and leaf springs from old cars are very useful.

With this simple list you can fire up and start. You will quickly learn how to use these tools and what other tools and equipment that you will need. As you begin, I feel that it is important to work with the following in mind:

> Among mechanics, the blacksmith holds a unique position, he being practically the only one who makes his own tools. This he often does without any apparent aim at economy, beauty, or usefulness, if judged by the chunks of steel on the ends of handles to be found in the odd corners of a great many blacksmith shops. It would not be fair to put the whole blame on the blacksmith, as he is usually allowed but very little time either to keep his tools in repair or to make new ones; the result is that if ever blacksmith's tools have had a high standard of efficiency, they soon depreciate. Too much reliance seems to be put on the old saying: 'A good workman can do a good job with any kind of tools'. But when it comes to saving time, which is one of the most important points in modern manufacturing, the good workman with good tools comes out ahead. [James Cran, *Machine Blacksmithing*, p. 5]

Processes and Exercises

You have now made the commitment to become a blacksmith and have lit the internal fire of motivation. Keep it burning, supply fuel for it and tend it well. There may be discouraging periods that seem to smother this fire; they are nothing more than clinkers. The fire will continue to burn brighter than before once they are removed.

Lighting a Fire

The next step is to light the forge fire. Light the fire with the feeling that each time you forge, you will learn something new.

The first time you light a fire you will have to make coke (breeze). Pack a layer of wet green coal around the sides of the firebox. (Green coal is new, unburnt coal.) Then place some wadded newspaper and small kindling in the center. Light the paper and use a small blast to get the fire going; add a few more pieces of wood as the fire catches. When the wood catches, place some more coal around the edges and a few pieces in the center of the fire. Do not smother the fire with green coal or you will be smothered with smoke. The coal will soon catch on fire and begin to burn off the gases. Keep the blast going. (Notice that the flame consumes the smoke; cut the blast and watch what happens.) Gradually build up the banks of green coal on the sides and back of the fire, wet down all of the coal with the watering can and pack down the banks with a shovel. This packing and watering with the fire forms coke. The fines in the coal act like cement to bind together the larger pieces.

By now you should have a good fire and some coke. Cut the blast and check the fire with a poker. If the coal is sticking together on the sides, it is coke. If not, turn on the blast, pack the banks in closer to the center of the fire, and water it down again.

If you water down a new fire that has a lot of green coal in it, and do not have the blast on, you can cause a blow back. This is a dull pop or explosion of the unburned gases that have been trapped in the fire. This can damage your bellows and sometimes the blower. It is definitely not good.

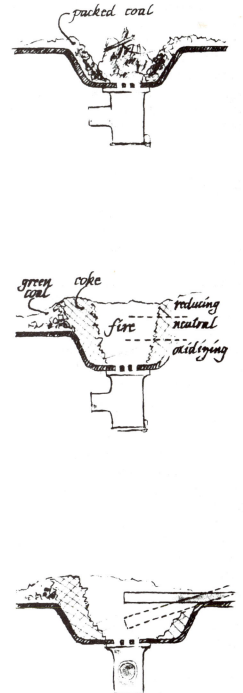

Each time you shut down, make certain you have enough coke set aside to start another fire. In time you will need only a little paper or wood shavings with the coke to start a fire. Your first fire should be the last fire that has a lot of smoke. A good smith is known by the way he starts, maintains, banks and shuts down his fires. This is something to work on.

Remove the ash and clinkers that form as the fire burns. A clean fire is essential. Dig around in the fire with the poker. Coke and coal will feel soft, but a clinker feels hard. It will clink. Clinkers are the dark areas in the fire. Try to remove them with the poker and pickup tongs. Rotate the fire grate or tumbler several times and dump the ashes. Move the bank of coke and coal closer to the center of the fire with the shovel or rake and turn on the blast. Add more green coal to the outer edge of the bank and wet it down. You now have a good fire, which will heat the iron more quickly.

There are three types of fires: reducing, neutral and oxidizing. The reducing fire is one that consumes all of the oxygen from the blast. It is a compact bed of coals and coke. The sides are well banked and formed, so that the heat is reflected inward, making a hotter and more desirable fire. The oxidizing fire has excess oxygen. It is usually hollow with a layer of coals and clinkers. It is impossible to weld in this type of fire and it is also more difficult to heat the metal. In a normal or neutral fire, scale forms and about 1 percent of the metal's weight is lost; in an oxidizing fire, this loss is much greater. Proper fire maintenance is not difficult. It takes time, but it saves time. Get in the habit of working with a good, clean fire.

Place the steel in the fire in a horizontal position, with a good bed of coals under it. It will heat easily, and have less tendency to scale (oxidize), because the oxygen is burnt off before it reaches the metal. In contrast, if you shove the steel down into the fire, the metal will scale more.

Cutting

The first piece that you work on will be made from ¼-inch round mild steel. We will cut it off cold. Place the hardie in the anvil and place the piece across the edge of the hardie. Using a hammer, strike the steel with direct, heavy blows. After several blows, rotate it and hit it on the other side. Notice the notches or nicks forming. When you are almost through the piece, slack off on your blows. The last blows will seem mushy and you can feel the metal give. Stop, and do not try to cut all the way through, since you might hit the hardie's edge and damage it. Now bend and break it in your hands, or stick it in the pritchel hole and break it off.

To cut a hot piece, place the bar in the fire and turn on the blast. Bring it to an orange heat.

Always cut the blast when you remove a piece from the fire, so that you don't waste fuel. Place the iron on the hardie and cut off an 18-inch piece. Notice how much easier it is to cut and how quickly the notches form. Slack off on your blows when you see a thin dark line appear on the bar. This is caused by the cooling action of the edge of the hardie. There are several ways to finish now: use shearing blows off the hardie or edge of the anvil; hold the piece on the face of the anvil and bend back and forth; or cool the piece in the slack tub and break it off. (The water hardens the metal, allowing it to snap off easily.)

Heat the end of this piece of iron to heats ranging from yellow at the end to a dark red. Then strike the bar with blows of equal force at intervals along the bar. Cool the bar and examine the difference in the marks made.

Drawing Out

Bring the 18-inch piece that you have just used to an orange heat. Remove the hardie from the anvil. Prepare to draw out a 4-inch-long square taper on the bar. Cut the blast and remove the bar from the fire. Place it over the anvil. This will give you a chance to check your stance and position at the anvil. Strike the piece with medium blows and gradually pull it over the edge. These blows will cause the iron to bend and will create a dimpling effect on the bottom. Rotate the piece 180° and do the same thing to the other side. This will straighten out the piece. Rotate it 90° and do the same thing to the other sides. The bar will be losing its heat by now, so place it flat on the face of the anvil, straighten it out and return it to the fire. Bring the piece to an orange heat and continue to

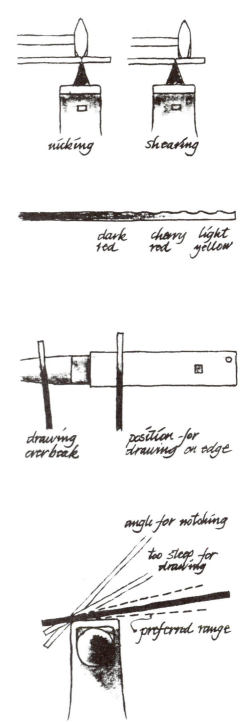

nicking   shearing

dark   cherry   light
red   red   yellow

drawing   position for
overback   drawing on edge

angle for notching

too steep for
drawing

preferred range

draw out, concentrating on the end, which will come to a sharp point. Occasionally lay it flat on the face of the anvil and hit flat blows to smooth out the dimples that have formed. Be careful not to let the dimples get too high or pointed.

Heat the taper again and prepare to finish it. Wipe the face clean of scale and draw out the taper on the face of the anvil, continuing to work as the piece loses its heat, until it is dark red. This is the finishing heat. Scale will not form now, and any scale that has already adhered can be removed by hitting the piece. Be careful to use light finishing blows. You should not try to shape the metal at this heat, because it is now losing its plastic quality. (This is particularly true when working tool steels; working them at this heat might crack them.)

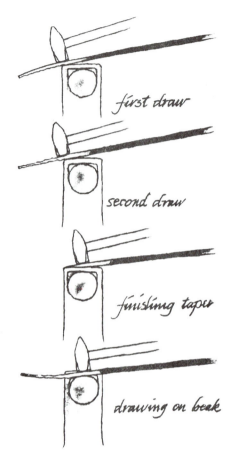

first draw

second draw

finishing taper

drawing on beak

Cool the taper and place the other end in the fire and prepare to taper it by tumbling. Rotate the piece 90° on the edge of the anvil after the first blow. Then rotate it 90° back to the original position and strike it. This makes drawing out faster and easier. Develop a cadence or rhythm to your blows. (A good smith can be heard as well as seen.)

Bring the piece to the proper heat and place it over the edge of the anvil; hit and rotate, hit and rotate, hit and rotate. Do this until the end is reached. Then change the position of the bar in your hand, so that you strike the other two sides. Develop a square taper as before and finish off.

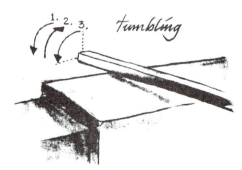

tumbling

This is the basic operation of drawing out. It will be used many times. To ensure drawing out properly, dress the edge of the anvil as discussed in section II.

Hooks

You can make some hooks with the tapers just finished. Heat a piece to light cherry; be careful now, because the thin end heats more quickly and can easily burn. Start the bending blows as in a and continue as in b and c. This forms a small pigtail or loop on the end. The heat will soon be lost on the thin section. Turn the piece over and proceed to step d. Form a right angle as in e, and take care not to strike the hook at position 2., as this will weaken it. Now heat the piece to a light cherry, turn it over again and bend it over the beak of the anvil (f). (After you remove the piece from the fire, dip the pigtail in the slack tub. This cools the end, and you can hit it lightly with the hammer without deforming it.) You can make any size hook, depending on where you place the hook on the beak of the anvil.

Heat the hook to cherry red and cut off the hook on the hardie about 1 inch from the right-angle bend. Holding the hook in a pair of suitable tongs, return it to the fire and draw a short taper for the nail end.

While the hook is still warm, rub it with an old candle or a piece of wax; then wire brush it. Place it over the fire to warm up again and rub it with wax again. This allows the wax to penetrate under the scale and to act as a rust preventative. Rub the hook with a cloth. When you install the hook, drill a lead hole into the wall.

It is important to follow this sequence of steps. There is usually an orderly procedure for each operation, although this is not always immediately apparent. Always plan the sequence in advance, particularly for complex parts.

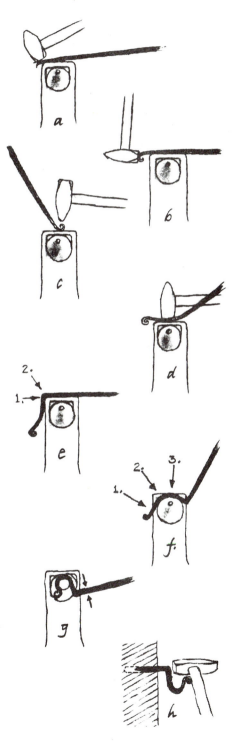

Examine your hook. It is your first piece. Note the qualities that you like and enhance those in your next hook.

The first steel that you worked with was light, so get a heavier piece and try a hook that is about ⅜-inch round. Proceed through the same drawing-out steps to develop the square taper. Instead of using the edge of the anvil to draw out this time, use the beak of the anvil. Obviously it has a much larger radius and gives a different effect. It will have a much different sound and response to the hammer, because it does not have the same mass as the body of the anvil.

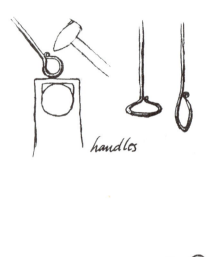

handles

Twisting

The next process is twisting. It is decorative and sometimes functional, as for example, when you make skewers.

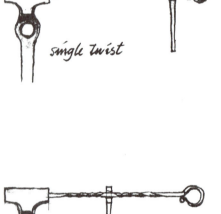

single twist

Cut off a 20-inch piece of ¼-inch square mild steel. Draw out one end and form a loop as in the hook exercise. Use the cross peen of the hammer to close the loop of the handle.

Taper the other end and prepare to twist. Set the jaws of your vise to the size of the stock. Heat the piece, moving it back and forth through the fire. The bar will be hotter in the center. It is possible to make more twists in the center, because it is softer. This gives a graceful movement to the piece. Clamp one end of the piece in the vise. Do not clamp it where it is hot, since this will mar the finish and will break the even flow of the spiral. After the piece is in the vise, twist the handle to form the spiral. Use gloves and have a brush handy to clean off the spiral, so that it can be seen.

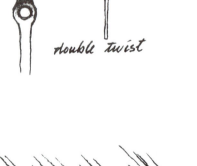

double twist

others sections to twists

To do a reverse twist, secure one end of the piece in the vise, and hold the handle firmly in one hand. With Vise Grips or pliers in your other hand, grip the metal in the center, and twist. Do not allow the piece to turn in your hand as you are twisting it in the center. Be careful that the skewer does not wobble and get out of line. If it does, you can straighten it out later on the face of the anvil. The sharp edges of the spiral will be softened, though.

Make a set of skewers with different handles and twists. When the set is complete, wire brush them briskly and finish them with an edible oil, such as vegetable or olive oil. This type of oil can be carburized over the fire by heating the skewer and then reheating after applying the oil. This slightly burns the oil; it is the same darkening action that takes place on your pots and pans.

Fire Rake

You can make a combination fire rake and poker with the techniques just described. This tool is handy for raking coal into the fire, breaking breeze and removing clinkers. Use ⅜-inch round stock about 24 inches long. Form the handle; twist the center section. Flatten the rake end by bringing to an orange heat and laying it on the face of the anvil. Use heavy blows to spread the metal. Clean up the hammer marks and point the end. Bend the rake end.

fire rake

Simple Toolmaking

You will soon learn to appreciate the fact that in blacksmithing you can make many of your own tools. In these next exercises, you will

49

make a center punch, a cold chisel and a hole punch. As you do this, you will learn the basics of heat treating, which comprises three steps: annealing, hardening and tempering.

Try to find a discarded car coil spring from a garage or scrapyard. This steel has 60 points of carbon, is hard, tough and suitable for these tools.

When we make these tools, it is important to heat the steel evenly in a reducing fire. Rebuild your fire, if necessary. Heat the spring to a light cherry and straighten out a section about 24 inches long. Cut it off on the hardie and allow this piece to air-cool. (When you put aside a piece of hot metal, be certain that it is out of the way, so that you will not bump it or pick it up inadvertently and be burned.) Straighten out the remainder of the spring, cut it into 24-inch pieces, set them aside and allow them to cool. When the first section that you have cut off is comfortably cool to pick up, bring it to a light cherry, cut the blast and leave it in the fire to soak in the heat for a moment. It is important to heat heavier sections of metal evenly, so that no fractures occur while you are forging. If the metal is heated too rapidly, it will be hot on the surface and cooler on the inside; this condition will cause it to crack internally while you are working on it. If, however, the piece has cooled on the surface and is hot inside, surface cracks may form. Therefore, you must be careful to heat the metal evenly.

Study the temperature chart. The upper part of the chart indicates the incandescent colors or forging colors. These colors are used in the hardening step of heat treating. The lower part of the chart deals with the oxidizing colors or temper colors. These colors are used in the

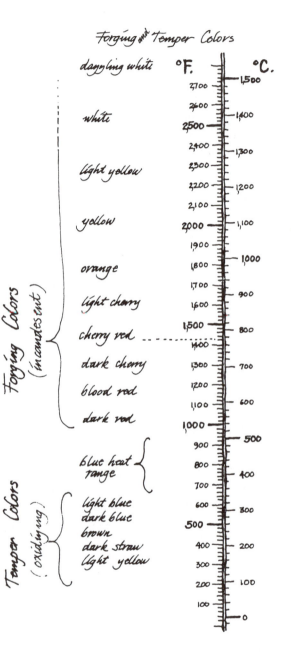

Forging and Temper Colors

Color	°F.	°C.
dazzling white	2,700	1,500
white	2,600	1,400
	2,500	
	2,400	1,300
light yellow	2,300	1,200
	2,200	
	2,100	
yellow	2,000	1,100
	1,900	
orange	1,800	1,000
	1,700	
light cherry	1,600	900
cherry red	1,500	800
	1,400	
dark cherry	1,300	700
blood red	1,200	
	1,100	600
dark red	1,000	
	900	500
blue heat range	800	400
	700	
light blue dark blue	600	300
brown	500	
dark straw light yellow	400	200
	300	
	200	100
	100	
		0

Forging Colors (incandescent)

Temper Colors (oxidizing)

50

tempering step.

After the piece has soaked in the fire for a moment, turn on the blast and bring it to a yellow heat. Draw out the end of the bar, forming a taper 2 inches long and about ¼ inch square. This is a test piece. With an old file, make notches ¼ inch apart. These are reference marks, enabling you to see the colors of the hot steel when it is quenched (cooled in water to harden). Heat the taper as indicated and look at the positions of the various colors on the taper, using the reference marks as a guide. Count the number of marks back to cherry red and dark cherry, since this will be the temperature range at which the piece will be quenched. It may be necessary to return the taper to the fire, if all of the heat has been lost while you were studying the colors. When the piece reaches these colors and you can visualize them clearly, quench the piece by plunging the taper into water and swirl it around until it is cool. The piece has now been hardened.

Now we will look for the section that is in an optimum crystalline state. Place the first notch over the edge of the anvil and tap a shearing blow to the end. The piece will fly off easily. Examine the broken end and notice the granular quality. This is the crystalline structure of the steel. Move to the next notch and break it off; notice the differences in the crystalline texture. It will be finer. (Keep the pieces and line them up.) Do you remember the colors at these points? Continue the process until you reach the piece with the finest crystalline structure, which will appear as a fine dull grey color. It also will break unevenly. Remember what the color was at that point, as this is the "critical temperature" for this steel.

Center Punch

You can now make a center punch with this piece. Since it is already drawn out, form a good taper which has a point that is ¼ inch in diameter, cut off a 5-inch section and chamfer the end. To bring the piece back to round after the taper is formed, develop the square section into an octagonal section and then forge it into a round section. If these steps are not followed, or a proper heat is not used, internal fracturing can result.

The forging process is finished and the steel should be annealed.

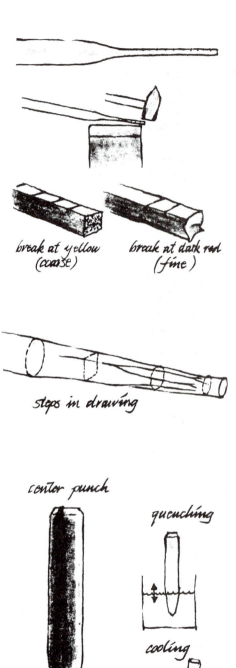

break at yellow
(coarse)

break at dark red
(fine)

steps in drawing

center punch

quenching

cooling

Heat Treating

Annealing means heating the metal to the critical temperature and cooling it by burying it in a dry medium, such as ashes, lime or sand. (Allow the metal to heat evenly and do not overheat the piece, or this will enlarge the crystalline structure and weaken the piece.) It is annealed when it is cool enough to pick up. This will take some time, so go on to make some other tools of the same material.

After annealing, heat treating is usually carried out in two different operations, which are hardening and tempering. It is sometimes possible to harden and draw a temper in one operation. Lay the tool on the fire with the punch end near the edge. You do this so that the thin part will not overheat. Heat it evenly and slowly, bringing it to the critical temperature previously determined by the hardening test. With a pair of tongs, grasp the center of the punch. Plunge the end into water about 2 inches deep, gently swirl it around and move the punch up and down about an inch to prevent a water crack.

The metal is hardened. Hold it for about 5 seconds and then quickly polish the end, using an emery cloth, sharpening stone or bench grinder. The oxidizing colors appear on the surface of the bare metal.

Study the chart of temper colors. (See page 116.) The second stage of heat treating is drawing a temper. The cooler part of the punch is now being warmed by the hot part and a thin layer of oxide is forming on the surface of the bare metal. As the hardened part heats up, this oxide film changes color from faint yellow to blue. This color change is an indication of the temperature of the steel; when the punch becomes purple, you should quench it again. The end is now tempered; this is where we get the term, drawing a temper.

Change the position of the tongs and quench the head for a few seconds in a depth of 1 inch; this slightly hardens the head. Stand the punch end down in a can of water 2 inches deep and allow the punch to cool completely.

Punches and Chisels

You can make other punches and chisels with the remainder of the spring steel. Refer to the diagrams and charts for sizes and tempering colors. The colors will draw faster when you are tempering these tools, because there is additional heat in the longer shank. You must work fast. Each of these tools should be dressed according to its use and need. When you are using the bench grinder, don't overheat (this will take out the temper you have just put in); cool the tool in water frequently.

You might want to refer to section IV and read "Metallurgy for the Blacksmith," which will

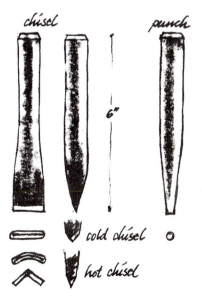

chisel   punch

6"

cold chisel   o

hot chisel

explain in more detail the processes that you have just completed.

While you are dressing the tools, bank the fire so that it will be ready when you return. Rake the coke in a mound over the fire and cover it with some green coal. (Or, bury a block of wood in the center of the fire and bank it.) This will assure a new supply of coke when you return.

Shutting Down

When you are shutting down for the day, you can let the fire go out, but this wastes a lot of fuel. It is better to pull the coke away from the fire toward the side of the forge, allowing the fire to die out. To fire up again, dump the ashes and light up.

Now that the fire is taken care of, plan your work schedule for the following day and design the pieces to be forged.

Upsetting

Upsetting is the process of making a piece of steel shorter and thicker. It is the reverse of drawing out. Sometimes upsetting is called "jumping up."

There are several ways to upset, depending on the size of the metal and its use. Upset short pieces on the face of the anvil. Hold the piece, hot end down, with tongs or gloved hand, and strike it on the cold end. In this way the heated part of the metal will be uniformly upset or thickened. (In contrast, when the heated end is struck with the hammer, only the very end of

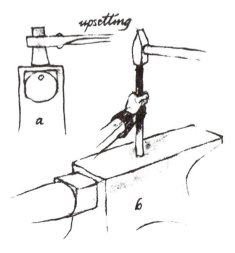

54

the heated part is upset or spread. This is called heading.)

When the end is gathered enough to hold on the edge of the anvil, you can strike it with "backing-up blows" to finish upsetting the end and to shape it. You will not be able to upset as fast this way, but you will have more control in shaping the piece.

Upset longer heavy pieces of steel against a heavy upsetting block or anvil placed on the floor. Ram the piece to be upset against the block; in this way, the combined weight of the piece and force of the smith upset the end.

Various stages in the upsetting process are illustrated in figure d: the metal is being upset normally in 1.; 2. and 3. illustrate some bends that must be straightened out before continuing to upset; 4. indicates the way in which a poorly upset end will curve under and be flawed; 5. shows what happens when light blows are used; 6. shows a bar which is upset in the middle, because the end was cooled before the bar was struck.

The end of the bar should be even and cut at right angles to the bar. Square up the end of the bar before you upset it. If the end is uneven, curves and bends will form in the bar and you will have to spend a great deal of time straightening it. After each heat, straighten out the piece before you return it to the fire.

Chain Hook

To make a hook, select a ½-inch round, mild steel rod and cut off a 12-inch piece on the cutoff hardie. (Or, you can roll the piece over the edge of a regular hardie as the piece is

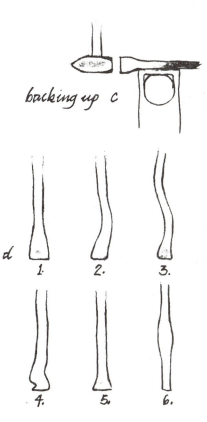

backing up c

d

1.   2.   3.

4.   5.   6.

struck to cut the end evenly.) Bring the bar to a light yellow heat and upset the end. As you strike the bar, look at the end you are striking, not the end to be upset. If you don't, you will miss the bar. Work surely and quickly, since upsetting requires more heats than drawing out.

The force of your blows will determine the shape of the upset. If you want to upset just the end, use light blows; if you want a longer length of upset, hit harder. Slightly chamfer the end if it is spreading too much. (Or, upset it in the step of the anvil by holding the bar at a 45° angle.)

When the rod has increased in diameter to about ¾ inch, form a ball on the end by holding the rod against the edge of the anvil and striking it with backing-up blows (or use the horn of the anvil). Bring the ball to a yellow heat and flatten it out until it is about a ½-inch thick.

Punch a ⅜-inch hole in the center. Bring the piece to a yellow heat and lay it down on the face of the anvil. Then drive the punch halfway through with four or five heavy blows. Cool the punch after two or three blows. Turn the piece over, and place it over the punch hole. There will be a slight bulge on the side that has just been turned up, and the metal will be slightly darkened (because of cooling). As you hold the piece over the punch hole, place the punch on the bulge and punch through. The slug will fall cleanly through the hole. (In contrast, if you punch the piece from one side only, a deformed hole will result (d). Shape this hole into an eye. Use the beak of the anvil or a mandril to form or enlarge the hole. Cut off the bar 8 inches from the eye and draw out the end. Shape the hook.

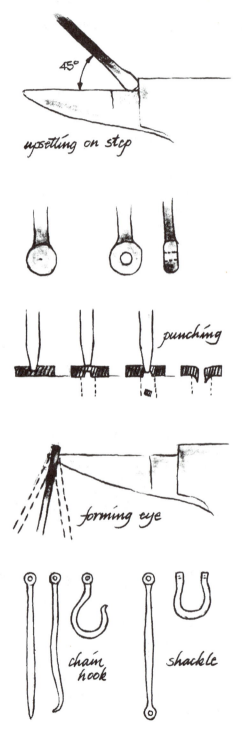

upsetting on step

punching

forming eye

chain hook

shackle

A shackle can be made in much the same way. Upset both ends, form a ball on each end, and punch each to form an eye. Then bend the bar into a U shape.

Spoon

You can now make a spoon. Sketch several spoons before you begin work at the forge, and then plan your work.

Use ½-inch mild steel (as you did for the hook) and form it in the same way, but finish it differently.

1. Upset the spoon end and form a ball, which you will flatten later. The final shape will be largely determined by the basic shape made at this stage.

2. Form the thin section of the handle where it joins the spoon.

3. Flatten out the spoon and shape it. (The spooning will be the last operation.) While the iron is still hot, use an old file to shape the edges and make the spoon symmetrical.

4. Shape the handle, blending it into the spoon end.

5. Form the spoon.

6. Finish with an edible oil.

There are two ways to flatten out the end of the spoon. Heat the metal to a light yellow and strike it with hard flat blows. Either spread the metal with a cross peen hammer at right angles to the peen, or spread it uniformly in all directions with the face of the hammer.

flattening

spreading

peening

sinking

There are two ways to form the spoon using a ball peen hammer. The first is called peening. Heat the metal to a bright cherry and strike it with the ball peen on the face of the anvil and form a cup shape in the spoon. Begin striking in the center, and work gradually in a spiral till you reach the outer edge. Use lighter blows on the edge. The result is a peened surface. The second method is called sinking. Place the spoon over the punch hole or in a swage block and sink the metal into a circular form. Do not hit the metal too hard, or it will stretch or buckle. You can make deeper forms more quickly this way. Whether you are peening or sinking, work in an even spiral, beginning in the center and working out to the edge. This prevents distortion and creates an even shape.

You can give final shape to the spoon when it is cold and can clean off the scale. If a great deal of cold work is to be done, the metal should be annealled occasionally. Anneal it by heating it to a cherry red and allow it to cool slowly.

There is another way to make a larger spoon or bowl from flats or sheet metal. Hammer the metal into a depression that has been carved in the end of a log or a block of wood. Use a ball peen hammer, forming hammer or wooden mallet to do this. Heat the portion of metal to be formed, place it over the depression and hammer it lightly. If you use a mallet with a rounded face, the bowl will be clear of hammer or peen marks.

You can also make a cupped form, such as a candle pan, from sheet metal by forming it over a stake. This technique is the opposite of the one just described, and is good for forming a lip on a bowl. Make a stake from a rod that is 1 inch in diameter. Round off the top and shape the bottom, so that it will fit into the hardie hole in the anvil or into a vise. Hold the sheet metal with tongs. Heat it, and place it on the stake. A dark spot will appear almost immediately on the top where the top of the stake cools the metal. Strike off to the side of the spot with the edge of your hammer, as you rotate the piece gradually. The metal will be gradually worked down. The edge of the hammer causes a slightly dented surface texture.

Candle Cup

Make a candle cup or holder by using the end of the stake to swage open the end of a ¾-inch tube. Heat the end of the tube and flair it over the end of the stake, by hitting it with light blows. Do not work the iron below a dark red, because it might split. Take several heats to get the tube to flair out. After the lip is formed and the metal is cool, place the flaired edge on the edge of the anvil and spread it further with a ball peen. Anneal the tube frequently when cold, working to prevent it from splitting. Cut off the cup with a hacksaw, when it is finished. Join the cup and pan together by brazing.

Many of these processes are quite similar to the techniques used by silversmiths. However, the iron is worked hot, while the silver is worked cold. It might be useful to study some books on silversmithing.

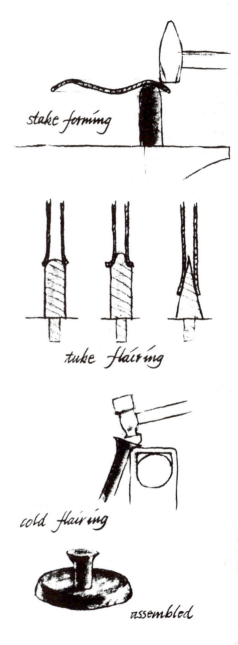

stake forming

tube flairing

cold flairing

assembled

Threading the Needle

Two other intriguing ways to treat the handles for spoons and spatulas are ''threading the needle'' and the spiral.

To thread the needle, draw out the handle end to a long thread of iron and punch a hole in the thick part of the handle. Holding the thread section with a pair of pliers, loop the end and thread it through the hole in the handle. Bend and twist the thread around the handle. Pliers with round jaws are the best for this job, because they do not mar the iron.

The Spiral

The spiral is a joy to make because it grows as you make it and is transformed in the last step as you pull it.

Sketch out the steps with a piece of soft aluminum or copper wire before you work with the hot iron. If you do this first, you will be able to work the iron without referring to the drawings, and you will be able to calculate the length of iron required.

Try it first with a piece of wire about 14 inches long and $1/16$ to $1/18$ inch in diameter. Clamp about 3 inches at the end of the piece in a vise. Bend the remainder at a right angle and quickly twist the wire counterclockwise. It is important to start properly. Remember that you must form both ends of the spiral in the same direction. You may have to reheat the wire several times as you make the spiral, because it tends to lose its heat rather quickly. Make about four complete twists, making sure that you close each turn tightly on the other; this ensures a round spiral.

Estimate the length of wire used to make the four twists, allow this much of the remaining wire to make another spiral and bend up the other end at a right angle. Heat this end and

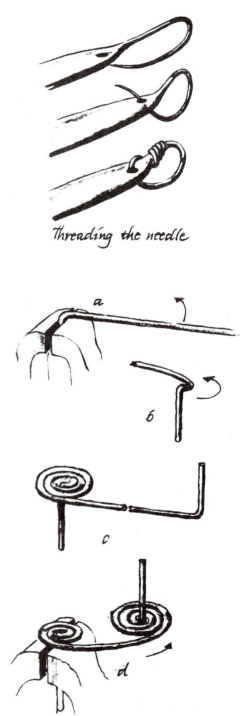

Threading the needle

60

clamp it in the vise. Then form another identical twist, making sure to turn in the same direction. As the last turn is made, the two spirals will lie on top of one another. Take an even light cherry heat, clamp one end in the vise, and with a pair of pliers, gently pull the other end. As you do this, the large turns will pull out easily; the tight ones can be helped with a pick or screwdriver. You can close up or adjust the spiral by lightly tapping the coil with a hammer as you gradually rotate it on the edge of the anvil.

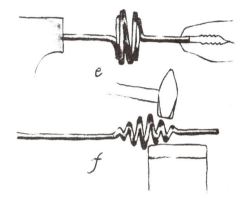

Heading

Heading is used to make nails, bolts and rivets. To head a rivet, strike the heated end, with the result that only the end is upset.

Make a heading tool first. This is a strip of tool steel which has a number of round holes of varying sizes punched into it. These holes are tapered and are larger in diameter at the bottom, making it impossible for the piece to jam in the hole. To make this tool, form a strip of metal and punch holes in it. Taper them with a tapered punch.

Then make a cupping tool. Grind a round point on the end of a bar that is ½ inch in diameter. This is the tool that will form the end of the cupping tool. Grind it to the shape of the head of the rivet. Clamp it in the vise. Next, upset the end of another bar ½ inch in diameter. Drive this onto the tool. This is the cupping tool.

The rivet set is the bottom companion to the cupping tool. It prevents the end of the rivet opposite the head from being flattened when the rivet is in place and you are forming the top of the head. Make the rivet set with a shank so that it can be held in the vise or hardie hole. Use the same bar with rounded end to form the depression in the rivet set.

Make several rivets 1 inch long and ¼ inch in diameter. Later you will need these for a pair of tight tongs.

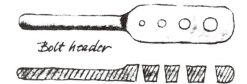

Bolt header

Select a ⁵/₁₆-inch rod and draw out about 1 inch of the rod to a ¼-inch diameter, using shouldering blows. Make it round. Rotate the rod over the cutting edge of the hardie and hit it with light blows. Do not cut it off; leave enough metal so that the rivet is still held on the rod.

Place the ¼-inch hole in the heading tool over the punch hole. Bring the rivet to an orange heat and place it in the heading tool. Break off the bar. Hit the top of the rivet quickly, so that it spreads evenly, and begin to form the head with the ball peen. After several blows, while there is still heat, use the cupping tool to shape the head. Then dip the header in water; the rivet will drop out, or can be lightly tapped out.

Do these things quickly to make the rivet in as few heats as possible. Think out the steps and then do them without wasted effort or motion.

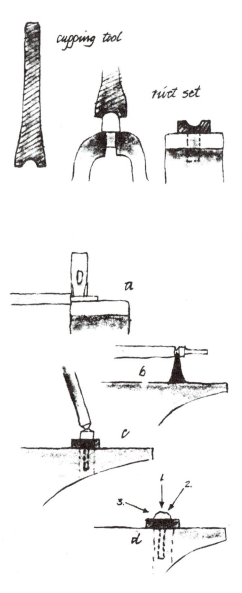

cupping tool

rivet set

> The time different smiths will be occupied over a given piece of work differs greatly. A smart smith will always do as much work as possible upon a forging in a single heat. While his iron is in the fire, he will mentally go through the sequence of operations, and see that whatever is required is at hand, and when the iron is on the anvil he will strike quickly while the iron is hot. [Paul N. Hasluck, *Smith's Work*, 1899]

Make up several more rivets and allow more

material for the head. After shaping the rivet, reheat it and place it in the header. Create different decorative patterns on the head with chisels or punches. Refer to some of the Yellin examples in section V.

Make a nail header with a square-tapered hole rather than a round hole, because a square nail is much easier to make. Make the hole slightly smaller than the nail stock. Form the header with a raised shoulder. This makes it easier for you to head the nail with angled blows of the hammer.

Nails

Nails are made in basically the same way as rivets. They are usually made from thinner square stock. Finish off the head with the hammer. This is a good opportunity for you to try to develop a rhythm and pace in your work. Time yourself; see how long it takes to make 10 nails. Look at your work patterns and the way in which you handled your tools. Do 10 more nails. Time yourself. How can you increase your efficiency? How many rods do you have in the fire? Can you do 60 nails an hour?

Upset rods of small diameter in the vise. Because they are thin, they have a tendency to bend if upset normally. Heat the rod, clamp it in the vise and strike it. The only disadvantage here is that the jaws of the vise will make sharp corners on the rod as they grip it. This can be avoided if you use a spring header inside the vise to clamp the rod.

Welding

Successful blacksmithing depends on many techniques. An important one is forge welding.

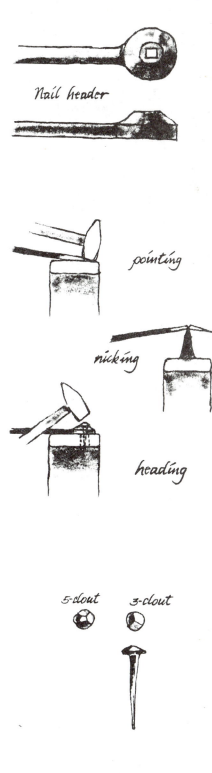

Nail header

pointing

nicking

heading

5-clout *3-clout*

Processes and Exercises

See how confident you feel after doing your first good weld.

When ferrous metal is heated gradually, it softens as the temperature increases and reaches the point at which two pieces of metal can be joined together by means of pressure or hammering. This cohesive union is called welding. The temperature at which this is possible is called the fusion point, or a welding heat. This temperature varies according to the alloying elements, particularly carbon.

Iron properly welded in the forge will have no visible joints, because of the cohesive bond of the crystals.

Successful welding depends on the following: an understanding of the process, a knowledge of the material to be welded, the correct flux, a proper fire, preparation of the parts to be welded, correct welding procedures and the refinement of the grain after the weld has been made.

Wrought iron is the easiest of the ferrous metals to weld, because it is almost pure iron. Its welding temperature is very high and the scale melts before the welding heat is reached. As a result, no flux is needed.

Steels with a small amount of carbon are easy to weld, and those with high carbon content are more difficult to weld. As the carbon content of the metal increases, the welding temperature decreases. This brings the metal dangerously close to the burning point. And, at lower welding temperatures, the melting point of the scale will be too close to the welding temperature, causing the scale to build up.

Flux

To prevent this, use a flux when you are welding high carbon steels. Flux serves two purposes: It combines with the scale and lowers the melting point, and after the scale melts, it forms a liquid barrier over the iron, preventing further oxidation (scaling). Use flux sparingly for the following reasons:

1. If you use too much, it will cause more scale formation rather than less, by attracting oxygen.

2. If there is too much flux in the weld, and it is not completely forced out by the first welding blows, it will form a barrier between the pieces to be welded.

Flux is not a glue. Welding is a process of cohesion, not one of adhesion.

There are a few good commercial fluxes available, and in addition, there are many formulas for flux. The basic ingredients are clean sand and borax. Clean sand is a good flux for mild carbon steels. When 4 parts sand and 1 part borax are used, the mixture becomes a general-purpose flux. Ordinary borax contains water, and when it is heated, it bubbles, melts and runs like water. After it cools, it is called borax glass (anhydrous). When this is pulverized and mixed 4 parts to 1 with sal ammoniac (ammonium chloride), the result is a good flux for carbon steels. Another good flux for high carbon steels is 50-percent anhydrous borax, 25-percent boric acid and 25-percent silica sand.

Iron filings are sometimes combined with flux. This serves two purposes:

Processes and Exercises

1. As the iron approaches welding temperature, the iron filings will be burnt off first, preventing the pieces to be welded from oxidizing.

2. Then when you hammer the pieces together, the filings will be forced out of the scarf faces, carrying away the scale and flux.

A reducing fire is necessary for welding. It should be made up of a deep bed of coals, and a cover of fuel over the pieces to be welded. (This prevents oxidization.) Heat the metal slowly in the fire to make sure that it is heated evenly. The blast should be low and steady; if necessary, the blast can be increased slightly just before removing the piece, to bring it up to welding heat.

Chambered Fire

There are several different types of fires for welding. The first one that we will use is a chambered fire. With this fire, you will be able to look into the fire and examine the piece as it heats. Start the fire as you normally would and make plenty of coke. Use a lot of coal in building up the banks and pack it down hard. After the fire is well made, place a 3-inch piece of 2 x 4 on top of the coals. Turn on the blast, add more wet coal over the block and build up the pile to make a roof over it. The wood will burn away, leaving a hole in the center. The coal will soon coke and form a roof that will support itself. Leave a small opening in the front. After you place the piece to be welded in the fire, you may want to cover the opening with a block of coke or a piece of sheet metal, since the full hot blast will come out of this opening. It helps to wear a glove, because this blast will heat up the full length of the piece.

chambered fire

Edge of the Anvil

Before you weld two pieces of metal, you must shape them, so that they will blend together easily. This is called scarfing. The scarf should be thicker than the rest of the piece, because the iron will be thinned out when the pieces are hammered together. The convex shape of the scarf face is critical. When you hammer the two pieces together, the scale will be forced out. The scarf faces must always touch in the center, not at the edges. (Flat pieces and bars are easier to weld than round pieces; rounds have a tendency to slide off one another when they are struck.)

scarf of loop weld

Our first weld will be an eye weld. Make the scarf on an 18-inch bar of ½-inch by ⅜-inch mild steel. Upset the end so that it is 1½ times the size of the stock, and then form the scarf using backing-up blows. The face should be convex and the end should come to a blunt point with a thin edge. Now bend the loop to form the eye at the end of the bar.

forming scarf

Place it in the chamber of the fire and bring it to an orange heat. Remove it from the fire and quickly sprinkle on the flux. Return it immediately to the fire. (At an orange heat, scale flakes away from the iron, allowing the flux to combine easily with the newly formed scale. At a cherry red heat, the scale adheres tightly to the iron and forms a barrier. Therefore always add flux at an orange heat to get the maximum benefit of the flux.)

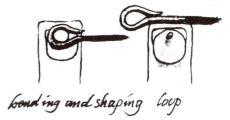

bending and shaping loop

Turn on a low blast, making certain that the weld area is in the center of the fire. You may have to push the piece through the fire to locate it properly. When the piece reaches a light yellow heat, turn it over so that the weld faces down in the fire. Be careful not to get dirt on the weld.

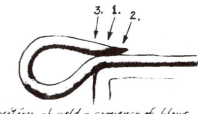

position of weld - sequence of blows

As the piece approaches welding heat, the flux will flow and form a smooth coating over the weld area. The iron will come to welding heat shortly after this, and the piece will be a light yellow. (It is bright and difficult to look at.) The surface will have a greasy or glassy appearance. When a few sparks start to come from the fire, it is at welding heat!

Your eyes may adjust to the bright light of the welding fire, and you may be momentarily blinded when you shift your attention to the anvil. Don't stare directly into the fire for long periods of time, for this reason. You might want to try sunglasses for the first welds; they will prevent the blinding and will enable you to see the fire more easily. You should wear safety glasses, because there will be a cascade of sparks when the weld is struck. I use a pair of safety glasses with industrial-weight ''Thermonon.''

The anvil should be clean of scale. Place the hammer nearby. When the piece comes out of the fire, you should know exactly what you are going to do, and it should be done without hesitation. Don't waste time, because the piece will cool quickly. Don't stop and look at the piece. Hit it!

Remove the piece from the fire, and as you are moving to the anvil, flick the piece like a paintbrush. (Or, you can tap the piece on the side of the anvil.) This will throw off any dirt which might be around the weld. Place the piece on the anvil and strike the blows as numbered. The first blows to close the weld should be light and quick; gradually make them heavier. Turn the piece on its side and work the sides. When the piece cools to an orange heat, wire brush each side quickly and sprinkle on some more flux, and return it to the fire. Bring it to a welding heat. Finish off the weld by continuing to work the sides and blending the eye with the stock. Two or three welding heats should be enough to finish the weld.

Welding greatly enlarges the grain size of the metal and therefore weakens it. When you are shaping the eye, continue hammering over the entire weld area until the piece cools to a dark red. Use light finishing blows. This is called "hammer refining." It reduces the size of the grain and restores the metal's original strength.

Make a weld on the other end of the bar, making the eye 1½ inches in diameter.

If the welds do not hold, examine the weld areas. If the eye was partially welded, only part of the weld was at welding heat. If there are dark spots in the weld area, there was dirt or flux in the weld, or the fire was oxidizing, preventing cohesion. If the metal is pitted and has a mottled look, it is burned. Cut it off and start again, being more careful this time.

Fire Poker

You can make a fire poker with the piece that has just been welded. Cut one loop with a chisel and shape the poker end to a point. Then form the hook end over the beak of the anvil. Shape and finish the poker halfway up the handle, cool it and work on the handle end.

Examine the bed of coals. The level of coals is now considerably lower, because the fire has burned down. Look for clinkers and remove them, rotate the tumbler or grate, and dump the ash. Clean the fire and add more fuel. You can add hard coke or hard coal to this fire now.

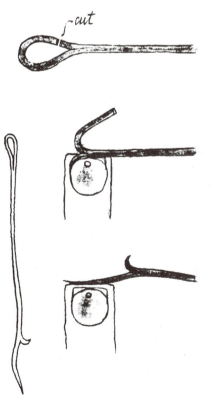

Both are good fuels, but you should not use them when you are starting a fire. Add them only when the fire is going and use breeze along with them. Many smiths turn aside when hard coke or hard coal are mentioned, but they have their place, particularly if it is difficult to obtain soft coal. The metallurgical or hard coke is useful for welding because it burns long and clean.

Open Fire

There is another type of fire that can be used for welding. It is called an open fire. After you clean the fire, break up the top (the roof of coke), and allow it to burn, while you build up the sides of the fire and pack them down again. Break the breeze into small pieces so that the work can be moved easily through the fire. It takes more experience to weld with this type of fire, but after a while, you will find it is the best. This is because the metal is completely surrounded by fuel and is protected from scaling.

Faggot Weld

It is sometimes difficult to get a feel for all of the variables in welding. Try the faggot weld. This weld will bring a mass of steel to the end of a bar more quickly than upsetting it would. Bend over 2 inches of a ¼-inch by ½-inch bar and double it back. Place it in the fire and bring it to an orange heat. Sprinkle flux on each side of the weld and return it to the fire. Bring to welding heat, fling away the dirt, and make the weld.

faggot weld

Try another faggot weld, but scarf the end and compare the welded area.

Welded Fork

Cut off an 18-inch piece of ⅜- or ¼-inch square mild steel to make a large welded barbeque fork. Scarf the ends, form the eyes and make loop welds on each end. If you are working in an open fire, gently lift the piece to see if it is at welding temperature. Do not move it around more than necessary or you will get dirt in the weld area. Welding temperature has been reached when there are sparks in the fire. The sparks will appear sooner if you are using a flux that contains iron filings, so judge the welding temperature by the surface appearance of the steel.

Cut the larger eye in half and draw out the tines. Then straighten and smooth them on the face of the anvil. Bend the tines over the beak.

Splitting

Splitting is the process of cutting with a chisel. Hot and cold chisels make a bevelled cut, but a cutoff chisel gives a straight cut. It is useful to work with a chisel when you are making forks, spoons, spatulas and hinges.

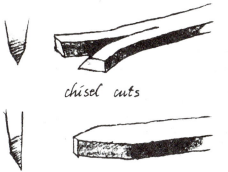

chisel cuts

Hinges

The butt hinge is named for the two pieces that mate or butt together and are joined by a pin. Make the hinge from a ⅛-inch by 2-inch or wider, mild steel bar. Form the strap before you work on the eye. Practice splitting and the techniques that you have learned.

To start the eye of the hinge, bend a small section at the end of the piece down over the edge of the anvil. Turn the piece over and continue forming the eye with backing-up blows. Just before the eye closes upon itself, insert a piece of round stock (or a nail) into the eye, and continue rolling the eye around the pin. Tighten up the eye with the cross peen hammer. Form the eye for the other side of the hinge in the same way.

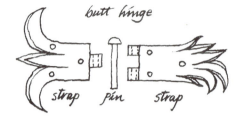

To butt the hinges together, cut out the center section of one eye and the end sections of the other eye. Line up the hinges and mark both with a file where the cuts will be made. Cut out a section in the middle of one of the pieces. Do this with a hacksaw, if the metal is cold, or with a chisel if the metal is hot. (Use a chisel with a flat side, so that it will make a vertical cut.) Cut the ends from the other piece. If you use a chisel to do all of the cutting, heat the piece to an orange heat with the pin in place, so that the chisel does not smash the eye. Keep the chisel cool by dipping it in water frequently. Then dress up the cut with a file to ensure that the two sections fit together properly. Place the pin through both eye sections to join them and cut the pin off allowing enough extra iron to form the head.

To head the pin, heat to an orange heat and quickly place it through the eyes of the hinge. Start to form the head, using a ball peen hammer and striking the pin with light, fast blows. The pin will quickly lose its heat, so return the whole hinge to the fire, with the part that you are heading down in the fire. The headed part will heat much more quickly than the rest of the hinge. You will be able to finish it easily now. Rotate the hinge. If it is tight, return it to the fire, bring it to a cherry red and rotate it again to free it.

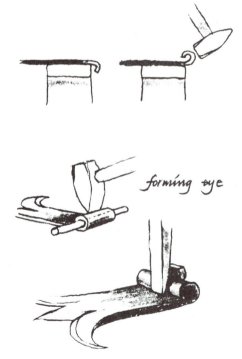

forming eye

You can also head the pin for the hinge with a gas welding torch while the pin is in place.

Pintle Hinges

The pintle is another type of hinge. It is made up of a pin that is hammered into the door jamb and another pin at right angles on which the strap rotates. The strap is made in the same way as one side of a butt hinge.

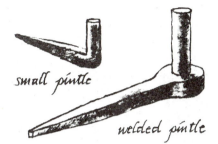

small pintle

welded pintle

If you are making a small, lightweight pintle, draw out one end of a piece of stock to make the pin and then make a right-angle bend. It is best to make a welded pintle, if you are making a large hinge for a heavy door. The welded loop of this type of hinge provides a large, flat bearing surface for the strap to rotate on. Prepare the scarf, bend the loop around on the back and make the weld. Insert a headed pin in the loop and weld it in place.

scarf for pintle

Clean up the pin with top and bottom swages and then form it in a header in order to clean up the bearing surface.

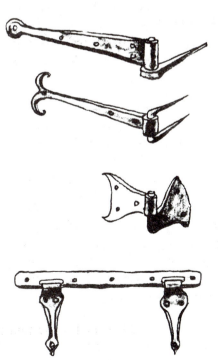

Processes and Exercises

Split Fork

You can also make a large fork by splitting
rather than by welding. Compare the drawings
of the two different types and you can select
whichever form suits your needs.

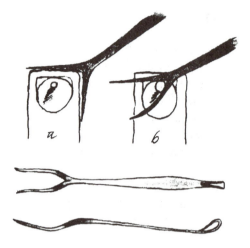

Make the split fork as follows:

a. Cut off a length of ½-inch by ¼-inch stock.

b. Flatten the fork end slightly.

c. Drill a ½-inch hole and split with a hot
   chisel.

d. Shape the neck and half of the handle.

e. Spread the tines and draw them out.

f. Shape the tines and neck. (This end is now
   finished.)

g. Shape the handle and finish the fork with a
   suitable oil.

h. Make a hook to hang the fork on.

When you are working with thin sections of
metal, such as tines of a fork, be careful not to
burn them. Turn the blast on only for a moment
and watch the points carefully. Sometimes it is
necessary to cool the points in the slack tub
and return the fork to the fire to heat the
heavier sections.

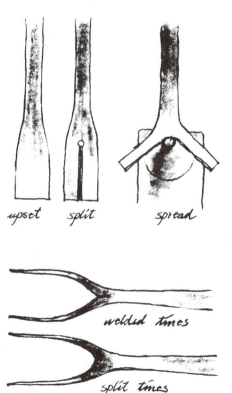

Fullers

The fuller is a basic tool that is used to start many forming operations. It has a rounded nose that is either straight or bent. With it, you can notch or spread out the iron; in other words, you can change the cross section of the iron. Sometimes you can use it to change the direction or axis of the metal.

Make a handheld fuller in much the same way that you would make a chisel, except that you upset the end and then shape it to a round end.

A simple spring fuller is handy. To make a spring fuller, cut off a ½-inch piece of round stock, 36 inches long. Flatten out about 8 inches in the center of this piece, till it is ¼-inch thick. Bend this center section into a circle about 4 inches in diameter, and bring the ends of the piece together, forming jaws that are about 1-inch apart.

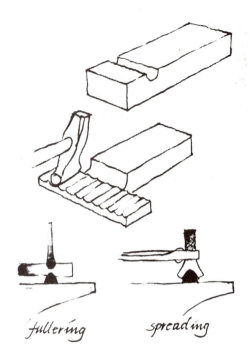

fullering   spreading

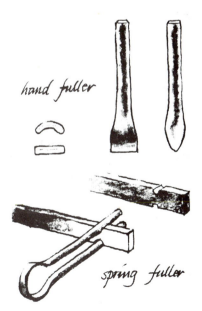

hand fuller

spring fuller

75

Trowels

Make trowels, spatulas and garden spades as
follows: Notch a flat bar of metal with the
spring fuller and then draw out this end to make
a shank for the handle. Make an offset bend in
the shank. To make the blade of the trowel,
grasp the shank with tongs and hold it upside
down on the inner edge of the anvil. Flatten it
on one side with heavy blows. Heat it again and
flatten out the other side standing at the other
end of the anvil. As you do this, a rib will form
on the top of the blade. Continue to flatten and
spread the blade. Trim the blade to the shape
desired. Recheck the thickness of the blade.
Make a wooden handle and fit it to the shank.

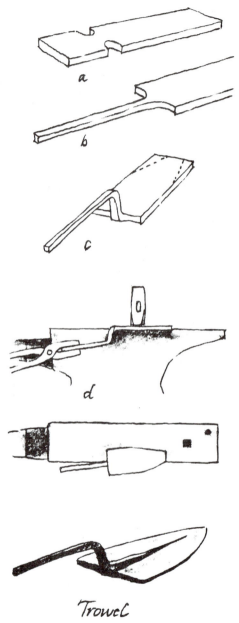

Trowel

When the iron is first roughed down, its
surface will not be smooth, though a good
smith can impart a very fair finish to a flat
surface by the hammer alone. The hammers should strike so as to bruise the work
as little as possible. There is a knack in
using the hammer so that its edges will not
mark the work, the blow being given by
the central rounding portion of the face
only. Striking fair with the middle of the
hammer face, each mark serves to partly
obliterate others, and leaves a very smooth
surface, only slightly wavy. This is all that
a smith working single-handed can effect
by way of finish. With the assistance of a
hammerman the surface can be smoothed
more effectually by means of a flatter,
which is held with the right hand of the
smith, and slid in turn all over the surface
of the work while the hammerman strikes
it with the sledge. Thus finished, the work
is left very smooth. [Paul N. Hasluck,
Smith's Work]

Swages

A swage is used to give the metal its final form, after a piece of metal has been partially shaped with other tools. Swages are frequently used in matched pairs. Like the fullers, they can be spring mounted for the single-handed smith.

To make the bottom swage, use a square bar the size of the hardie hole; upset it and cut it off. Bring it to a yellow heat, place it in the hardie hole and form it with a sledge into a rectangular block. Square up the sides. Bring it to a yellow heat, lay a ¼-inch round rod over the center of the block and using a hammer, form a groove in the swage that is about half the depth of the stock used.

To make the top swage, upset a bar to match the bottom tool. Make a groove in the top swage to correspond to the one in the bottom. Prepare a ¼-inch U-shaped rod that will wrap around the heel of the anvil. Place it upside down in the groove of the bottom swage. Bring the face of the top swage to a yellow heat, place it over the U, and hammer the swages together. This forms a groove in the top swage to match the one in the bottom swage. File off the edges of each swage so they do not pinch the metal. Temper the swages to blue if you are using a tool steel.

These tools can be used most effectively to shape the leg of a rivet rather than trying to make it round with a hammer.

Tenons

A tenon is a bolt-like extension at the end of a metal rod that serves as a connecting piece. You can make a tenon with the swages just

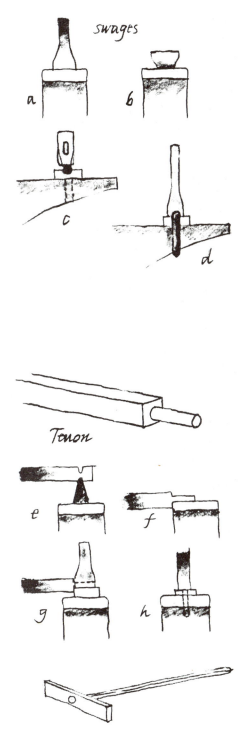

finished. It, in turn, will be used to make a
T square for the forge. Use a ⅜-inch square bar.
Either place the bar on the edge of the anvil and
draw out the end with a hammer, or notch the
piece with a small fuller (about $^1/_{16}$-inch
round). (This is sometimes called a veiner.)
Then draw out the end to form the tenon. Bring
the tenon to a light cherry, place it between the
swages and strike them with a hammer to shape
the tenon. Then place the tenon in a ¼-inch
header and strike it to square the shoulder.

To make the T square:

a. Use an 8-inch piece of ½-inch by ¾-inch
   mild steel for the head.

b. Punch a square hole in the center of the bar.
   This will prevent the head of the T square
   from rotating.

c. Cut the tenon ⅞-inch long with a hacksaw,
   and bring it to a light cherry.

d. Hold the main part of the T square upright,
   and place the tenon into the hole in the
   head piece. Strike the tenon with a hammer, using heavy blows. This will form a
   head on the tenon.

e. Square up your T square with a carpenter's
   square, and peen the tenon till it is flush
   with the head.

Drifts

Drifts are forming tools that are used to shape a
hole after it has been punched or drilled. Form

the drift into whatever square or round shape that you want the hole to be and then drive it into the hole while the metal is hot. Drifts are usually so plain and simple looking that they are mistaken for scraps or unfinished pieces.

To make a square hole in a bar (as for the T square): Punch the hole with a punch. Punch the square drift through the hole and dress up around the hole. Leave the drift in the hole when you are working around it.

Eye Punch

An eye punch is a tool that is used to start the eye of a hammer. Then the eye drift is used to give the final shape to the eye. The eye punch may or may not have a handle. The handle is usually set at a 45° angle to the line of the eye because this makes it easier to see when punching a hole. Use an eye punch that is about 50 percent smaller than the final size of the eye, so that you do not remove too much metal during the punching. Then the drift is used to open the hole. It is absolutely critical that the punched hole be centered and perpendicular to the stock. If an eye punch is not available, and you are making a small hammer, use a drill press to drill the hole.

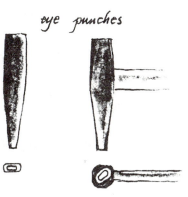

eye punches

You can make a simple eye punch and drift from a coil spring. Use the same method that you used in making other punches. Hold the punch with tongs or Vise Grips when you are using it.

Place a bolster under the piece when you are punching if there is not a large enough hole in the anvil. Bolsters can be any size or shape.

Small Hammer

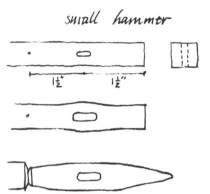

We will now make a small, straight peen hammer. With a center punch, mark off a piece of tool steel (80 points of carbon) for the head. Bring it to a yellow heat and punch the eye. After several blows, remove the punch and dip it in water to cool it; at the same time check the alignment of the hole. When the hole is about ¼-inch deep, dip the punch in a little coal dust before you return it to the hole. The coal dust will cause the formation of gases that will keep the punch from sticking in the hole as it is being hit. When you have punched the hole about three-quarters of the way through the head of the hammer, turn the head over and punch the hole through from the other side. Now, drive the eye drift into the eye. Leave the drift in as you work out the bulges on the sides of the head of the hammer. Draw out the peen. Make a cut three-quarters of the way through the bar at the face. Refine the shape of the head and cut it off completely. Bring the head of the hammer to the critical temperature and anneal it. When it is cool, dress the face and the peen with a bench grinder. The grinding removes the decarburized steel.

To heat-treat the hammer, take it to the critical temperature slowly, because the hammer is thick. Harden the face by dipping it in water to a depth of 1 inch; then turn the hammer and do the same with the peen. Quickly polish the face and the peen with emery and draw the temper on the face and peen to a light purple. Allow the eye to cool slowly. Dip the peen and the face alternately in water to allow the eye to cool slowly. Set the handle.

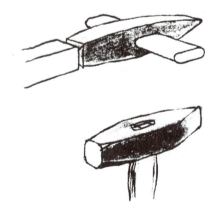

Rock Pick

You can make a rock pick, claw hammer or a striking tool with a long-sided eye using the following technique: Use 1-inch by 1½-inch tool steel. Punch a hole for the eye and open the eye with a drift pin until it measures 1-inch by ⅝-inch. Use a bevel set to form notches on each side of the eye. This forms a shank on the head. Draw out the ends to form the head and pick. Work with a drift pin in the eye when you shape the side of the eye, the head and the pick. Grind the face and the point of the pick. Harden the head and draw to a dark blue temper.

Set Hammer

Set hammers are used to "set" or form right angles and work the iron in tight spots where the face of the hammer could not make a clean hit. To do this, strike them with another hammer.

One might think that anybody knows how to make a set hammer, if every smith knows it, I don't know, but I do know that there are thousands of smiths who have never had a set hammer nor know its use. To make one: Take a piece of tool steel 1¼ x 1¼ inches, punch a hole about two inches from the end, the hole to be 1¼ x ⅜. Now cut off enough for head. Make the face perfectly square and level, with sharp corners, harden and cool off when the temper turns from brown to blue.

This is a very important little tool and for cutting steel it is a good deal better than the chisel. Plow steel of every kind is easier cut with this hammer than any other way. In cutting with the set hammer hold the steel so that your inner side of the set

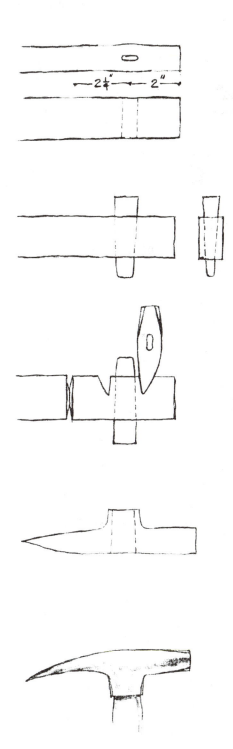

hammer will be over the outside edge of the anvil. Let the helper strike on the outside corner of the set hammer and it will cut easy. The steel to be cut should be just a little hot, not enough to be noticed. If the steel is red hot the set hammer cannot cut it. The heat must be what is called blue heat. I would not be without the set hammer for money, and still I often meet smiths who have never seen this use made of the set hammer. Plow points, corn shovels, and seeder shovels are quicker cut with this tool than any other way, with the exception of shears. [J. G. Holmstrom, *Modern Blacksmithing*]

When you cut steel with a set hammer, it is important to align the hammer and the edge of the anvil with a slight offset, which shears the iron cleanly, rather than pinching it.

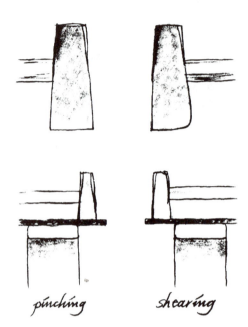

set hammers

pinching   shearing

Tongs

Tongs that are well made, that are easy to hold and that grip the iron well, will make your work much easier at the forge. Good tongs will last a long time and can be changed and reworked to do many jobs. Before each new job, adjust the jaws of the tongs so that they hold the stock properly. Then there will be no danger of the hot iron slipping out of the jaws and you will be able to proceed smoothly with your work.

There are many uses for small tongs at the forge. We will make several pairs, to get a feel for making tongs. These are easier to make than the heavy tongs explained later.

Study the detailed drawings of tongs and the steps involved in making them. These will help you to visualize the way in which tongs are made and assembled. Note that both pieces of the tongs are exactly the same. Draw one side of the tongs and then trace it. Turn the tracing over and place it on the original drawing; as you do this, you will see how the tongs mate and hinge.

Cut off two 12-inch lengths of ⅜-inch round mild steel. Upset one portion near the end of each piece (a). This is the hinge section and it should be heavier. Form the jaws and offset (b). Hold the handle at a 45° angle and turn the piece 90° to the left. Then flatten out the bulge section (c). Grade it into the handle. Turn the piece 90° again and form the S curve of the tong (d). Shape and refine this curve by means of shouldering blows. Draw out and taper the last one-third at the end of the reins. Make two identical pieces. Place them together and see how they match.

If the pieces are slightly different, rework them and true up on a bending fork (e).

Place the two pieces together to determine where the rivet will connect them. Mark the spot with a center punch and then punch or drill a ¼-inch hole in both pieces. You can place a ¼-20 nut and bolt in the tongs to check out their movement. You should make any necessary adjustments now before riveting.

Check the ¼-inch rivets previously made for fit and length. The length of the leg of the rivet coming through should be slightly over twice the diameter of the rivet. Heat the rivet to a yellow heat and place it in the tongs. Then put the head of the rivet in the rivet set so that it will not be flattened. Strike your first blow on the top firmly and quickly with the face of a small ball peen hammer. This blow will slightly expand the entire length of the shank of the rivet to the diameter of the hole. Strike the next blows quickly and lightly with the ball peen to

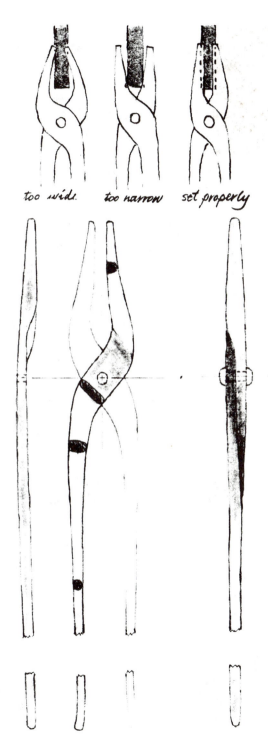

too wide.   too narrow   set properly

head the end of the rivet. Strike angled blows around the head of the rivet. When the head is partially formed, take the cupping tool and finish the rivet. This can be done in one heat with practice. If another heat is needed, put the tongs in the fire, bring them to a cherry red and finish the rivet. While the tongs are still red, open and close them to allow the faces and rivet to conform to each other. Adjust the jaws and reins to make sure they are aligned.

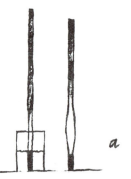

a

You can also make a pair of bow pliers using this process. These are useful as pickup tongs. Make the jaws on these 2½ to 3 inches long, round rather than square. The shape of the S curve in the throat should be more open. Use a drawing as a pattern for these tongs, as you did for the others.

b

Large Tongs

The size of the tongs that you can make by the previous method is limited because you have to upset the joint area and draw out the long section of the reins. You can make larger tongs using a lap weld, which is an overlap of two pieces and a very useful weld. And if you have a helper (a striker), you can make the tongs more quickly.

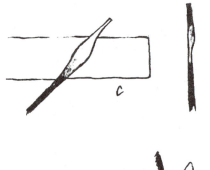

c

To make a pair of flat-jawed tongs, use ⅞-inch square mild steel. You will need about 4 to 5 inches for each jaw. They may be made from separate pieces or from opposite ends of the same bar.

d

First, fuller notches about ⅜-inch deep on the top and bottom of the bar with a top fuller. At a 45° angle, fuller another notch on the side that intersects with the top notch. Flatten the jaws and then spread the hinge area at a right angle

e

to them. Be careful to preserve the fillets formed by the fuller, so that the jaws are not weakened by sharp corners. Refine the shape of the jaws and form the inset or notch in the jaw with a square bar. This inset holds both square and round pieces firmly. Punch a ⅜-inch hole for the rivet. Then cut off the piece about 3 inches from the hole. Form a scarf for welding on the reins.

bow tongs

Lap Weld

Make the reins from a rod which is 14 to 15 inches long and a ½ inch in diameter. Prepare the rods for welding. But before you weld the tongs, practice with scrap stock. Cut off two pieces long enough to heat without tongs. Upset the ends, and make the scarfs, either with the edge of the anvil or with the cross peen. The scarf must be convex, formed at a 45° angle, and drawn to a point. The slight return on the end of the scarf will stay hot when the two are joined for welding.

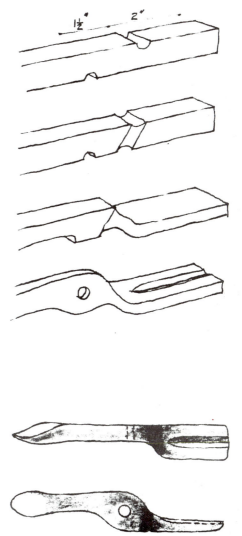

As mentioned previously, the fire must be a reducing fire that is clean and hot. Clean it out and prepare a deep, well-banked fire, if it is not. Clean the face of the anvil. Place a medium-weight hammer on the face of the anvil where you can grasp it easily and quickly. Plan your movements from the fire to the anvil and the way in which you will lay the pieces down on the face.

Place both pieces in the fire scarf down, so that no dirt will lodge there. Bring to an orange heat and add flux. Make certain that each piece in the fire is heating evenly. Pull one back if it heats too fast. Don't allow the pieces to touch, as they might weld together in the fire. When they have reached welding heat, come away from the fire and gently tap both bars, scarfs down, on the outer edge of the anvil in order to dislodge dirt. Place them quickly in position for welding. Hold the left piece scarf down and on top of the other piece to hold it down. Let go of the right-hand piece and grab the hammer. Strike the first blows immediately. They should be light, for heavy blows might knock the pieces out of alignment. Strike the second or third blow on the lip of the scarf to weld it. Turn the piece and close the other lip. Now strike increasingly heavier blows to close the weld and shape it. When the piece is at an orange heat, wire brush all scale off and quickly sprinkle a little flux on the weld line. Return it to the fire. Bring the piece to a welding heat and finish closing the weld by working around the weld lines. One or two heats should complete the weld. When you are finishing off, clean the face of the anvil and wire brush the piece. Any excessive scale will mar the finish.

Practice this sequence of welding several times before trying to weld the tongs.

If you are satisfied, try welding the reins and jaws of the tongs. You will notice that the jaws are heavier and will take longer to heat. Watch carefully. Hold the jaws with tongs in your right hand and the reins in your left hand. When you place the scarfs together, they will feel mushy and will tack together, so make certain that you align them properly. Drop the tongs immediately and pick up the hammer. Weld the jaws and reins together. Make certain to hammer refine the weld area. After both welds have been made, join the parts together with a ⅜-inch rivet and adjust the tongs.

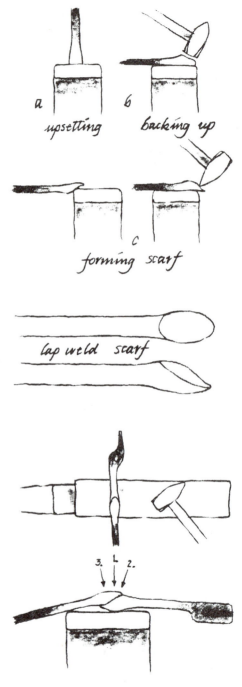

a upsetting   *b* backing up

c forming scarf

lap weld scarf

The Striker

The striker, or hammer man, is the smith's helper. He wields a sledge and stands opposite the smith at the anvil; he strikes the iron under the direction of the smith. The striker must be a knowledgeable smith for he must understand the way in which the hammer is being used and how much force is being applied. After each blow struck by the smith, the striker must hit the iron with his sledge in exactly the same spot, and at the same angle, but with a proportionately heavier blow. When striking, words are unnecessary; the language of the smith's hammer is the only direction needed. However, the smith must indicate when he wishes to start and stop. When he is ready to start, the smith will ring the anvil three times; when he is ready to stop, he will hit it to the side or will lay down his hammer, after the striker has hit his blow.

As he works, the striker must strive to emulate the force and direction of the smith's blows. Although he uses a heavy sledge, he should not try to hit as hard as he can. As the striker follows the smith's example, he becomes the alter ego of the smith.

Sometimes the smith will hold a tool, such as a punch fuller or flattie, in addition to the work. The striker will then strike the tool. Here also, the striker must know how to hit with the proper force and cadence, know when to start and stop and how to help at the forge. The striker also helps to maintain the fire, cut stock, get tools and organize things for the smith.

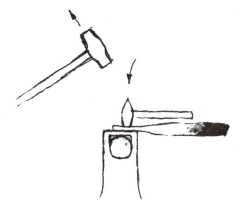

Sledges

There are two types of sledges that the striker uses. The first type is the hand sledge, which has a short handle (28 to 30 inches) and weighs from 5 to 10 pounds. Hold it with your right hand close to the head and raise it to the height of your head when you strike. Hold the end of the handle with your left hand. Do not slide or move your hands when you are striking. (This is called the up-hand position.) Although this position might seem awkward at first, you will soon find that it works well. Your right hand and both feet should be in the position that you use when you are striking with a hammer.

The second type of sledge is the swing sledge, which has a long handle (34 to 36 inches) and weighs from 8 to 20 pounds. Hold it and swing it like an ax, in a full arc. There will be considerable force created, but you will not have as much control. Sometimes more than one striker will be working, especially if the piece is very large. Then you will need a heavier, larger anvil.

When you are the striker, stand opposite the smith at a distance that will allow you to strike a good blow and then draw back slightly, as you raise the sledge and prepare for the next blow. Both the smith and the striker must work in rhythm as they alternate blows, being careful to keep hammer and head out of the way of the next blow. Your stance must be balanced; stand approximately as you normally would, but with a wider, more balanced stance.

Practice striking with a friend or fellow worker. In this way, you learn by doing. You will soon develop a rhythm. Drawing out is an excellent beginning exercise. Start striking and try to work in an even, steady cadence. Speed up slightly and then slow down. Try striking blows of different force and direction. Next, try tumbling while you are drawing out, keeping in mind that the smith must turn the piece before his blow only, never before the striker's blow. Otherwise, the striker would not know where to hit.

Anvil Tools

Anvil tools are much easier to make when you have a striker to help you. The extra force of the sledge offsets the difficulty of working with heavier sections of metal.

To make a hot hardie, select a high carbon steel that is from a ¼ to a ½ inch larger than the hardie hole. If you do this, you can easily form a shoulder on the tool to prevent it from jamming in the hole. (Use a truck axle, large spring or the teeth from a bulldozer blade, or use W 1 tool steel with 75 to 85 points of carbon.)

Fuller in on each side. Draw out the shank to fit the hardie hole. Place the shank in the hardie hole, and then strike the top with a sledge, thereby upsetting the shoulder and seating it. Make certain that the piece is perpendicular to the anvil when you begin. Also, rotate the piece 90° after four or five blows, so that it seats in all positions (c).

With your spring fuller, fuller a notch ⅜ inch from the shoulder (d). Cut off the piece 1½ inches from the shoulder. To finish the piece, hold it securely by the shank with a pair of close-lipped or square-jawed tongs. Draw out the

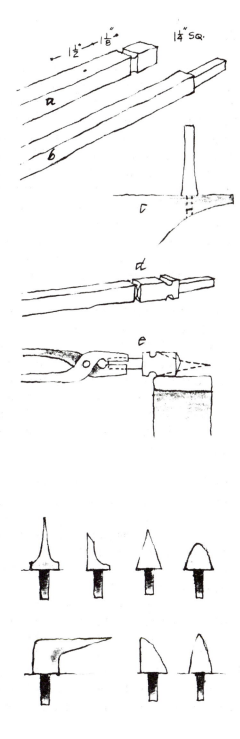

blade. Dress the cutting edge on a bench grinder.

It is best if these tools are annealed and then hardened and tempered. The cold hardie can be drawn to a purple, and the others to a blue.

Make the other anvil tools in the same way, but do not fuller a notch for the shoulder. Fuller only one side of the cutoff hardie.

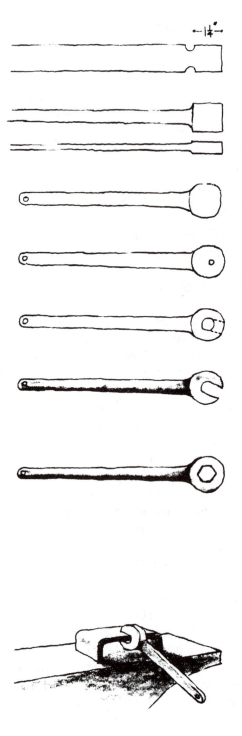

Wrenches

Open-end wrenches are very handy. You may want to make several of different sizes.

To make a ½-inch open-end wrench use a 1¼-inch by ⅜-inch mild steel bar. Form notches with your spring fuller in the wide section. Draw out the handle and cut it off at 6 inches. Form the handle and punch a hole in the end. Now turn to the head. Trim the corners of the head with a hot chisel and shape it to a circle. Punch a ¼-inch hole that is slightly off center; using a drift, and working from both sides, open the hole till it is a ½-inch in diameter. Cut a slot for the jaws at a 20° angle. Form the jaws on a saddle. Use a flatter to dress up the sides of the jaws. Use a file to dress up the jaws to the correct size. Carburize the wrench as described in "Metallurgy for the Blacksmith" in section IV. Carburization hardens the surface of the jaws, making them wear well and it preserves the tough core.

Make a closed-end wrench in the same way, but punch a ⅜-inch hole and form it with a hexagonal drift.

Knifemaking

There is not much forging involved in knifemaking, but there is a lot of bench work. It is rewarding, because during this process steel is brought to a highly refined form. The procedure can be broken down into the following steps: design, selecting the proper materials, forging, shaping and finishing the blade, heat treating, assembling the blade and handle, shaping the handle, final buffing and sharpening.

Decide what type of knife you need and make several sketches. Trace the shape of the blade onto a piece of cardboard, and cut out a blade template (or pattern). The template will serve as a guide at the forge for both the shape and the size of the knife. It is difficult to judge without it; because the blade always looks smaller at the forge (and in fact; may actually be too large).

Select an alloy steel that is tough, that will hold an edge, and can be forged. Knifemakers have found several tool steels that are excellent; these are W 2, F 8, O 1 and D 2 (see Tool Steels chart). Chromium and vanadium are two alloys which, in addition to carbon, will provide knives with edge-holding ability. When you buy tool steel, remember to get the manufacturer's instructions for heat treating and to follow them.

If corrosion resistance is important, the 400 series of stainless steels can be used. They are heat treatable, but 440 B and 440 C are the only ones that have sufficient carbon for knifemaking. Stainless has a very limited forging range, so you must be very careful when you are forging it.

Processes and Exercises

Old files and car springs may be used successfully. However, they lack the alloys mentioned above, and do not hold an edge as well.

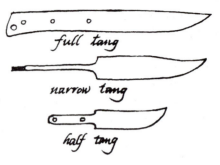

If you use a file, the teeth must be ground off first. Sometimes, because there is excessive sulfur in the steel, old files will crack when they are heated and forged. The steel is then called "hot or red short" and is not forgeable.

Make a half-tang knife by shaping the tang first. This is the narrow extension, which will later be enclosed by the handle. (Make it the length of a $3/16$-inch drill, because you will later drill a $3/16$-inch hole in the wooden handle.) Notch the metal with fullers and draw out the end, forming the tang. Be careful not to damage the radii formed by notching; they will prevent cracking during the heat treating later. Then punch the rivet holes in the tang. (The wooden handle will be attached to the tang by rivets later.) A half tang is not as strong as a narrow or full tang, but it is sufficient for a small knife.

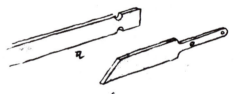

Now turn your attention to the blade of the knife. Bend the knife blade blank into a curve. The cutting edge is the edge on the inside curve. Strike this inside curved edge with a hammer, working from the tang on out; as the curved edge is flattened, it will gradually straighten out. At the same time, draw out and taper the blade. Use a flattie or a finishing hammer to refine the surface of the blade. Keep the scale brushed off. Make certain that the blade is straight, as this is the last of the forging operations. Anneal the blade.

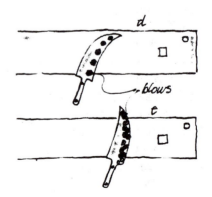

Remember that during the forging operations the surface of the blade will decarburize (i.e., lose carbon). This can be ground off during the shaping operations, but remember when forging the blade to use as few heats as possible and a reducing fire.

Place the template on the blade, and trace the outline on the blade with a piece of chalk. Grind the outline to shape. Check the taper and thickness.

The degree of finish that you use on the surface of the blade may vary from a highly polished one to one that has the forging marks left in. Finish the blade with a belt sander, which is better than a grinding wheel for this type of finishing. Shape, develop and finish the blade completely, but do not do the final buffing. This will be done after the heat treating.

After finishing the blade, heat-treat it in a fire of well-packed coke. You can also use charcoal or hard coal in the fire. Keep the blast low. A reducing fire will help prevent scaling.

Lay the blade on the fire and bring it up slowly to hardening heat. Turn it frequently. Be certain that it comes up uniformly and do not overheat it. Watch the point; it is thin and easily overheats. When the blade is at the proper color, quench it by placing it point down in the proper medium. (Check the tool steel guide charts in section IV for proper heat-treating information.)

When the blade is cool to the touch, temper it immediately. It is difficult to temper knives, because the blade is not uniform in thickness. A pot of oil makes a uniform tempering medium, but you will need a high temperature thermometer to take the temperature. You can also use an oxyacetylene torch to temper a knife. (Use a carburizing flame.) The torch offers flexibility, because you can move it over the blade and control the heat. (The flame is very hot, so work slowly and carefully.) Temper the parts of the blade differently. The tang and top of the blade should be the softest parts, the middle of the blade should be harder and the edge of the blade should be the hardest.

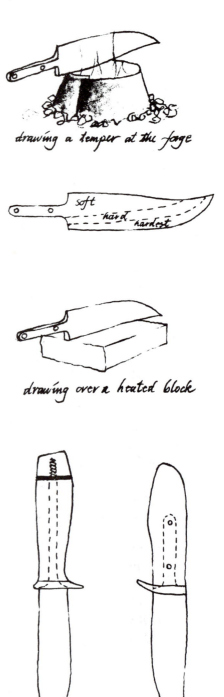

drawing a temper at the forge

To temper the blade in the forge fire, make a sheet-metal cone and place it in the fire. Temper the blade by moving it back and forth. (I prefer the fire to the torch since there is more control and less heat.) Temper colors for knives range from yellow to blue, depending upon the knife's use. Draw the temper on the tang to a light blue.

Another method of drawing a temper is to use a heavy block of metal that has been heated in the forge. Lay the knife on its back edge on the block and draw the temper. This is perhaps the safest method, but you must still be careful of overheating the point.

drawing over a heated block

There are limitless possibilities for your knife handle. If you want a knife guard, make it of brass or nickel silver. Both of these can be soft-soldered to the blade, if the soldering temperature is kept below the temper temperature. To make the handle, drill out the hole for the tang. Rough-shape the handle and drill out the holes for the rivets. Attach it to the blade with epoxy and rivets. Finish carving and sanding the handle.

When the handle is finished, you can buff the blade. Be careful not to overheat the blade (and thus take out the temper) as you are buffing it. Sharpen the blade on successive grades of oilstone, ending up with a hard, fine stone. The bevelled edge of the blade should form an angle of 15 to 20°, depending on the knife's use, and your own personal preference.

94

Chain

Chain links are made with a lap weld. Cut off some pieces, 7 inches long and ⅜ inch in diameter (one per link). Take one piece and bend it into a U shape, making sure that the legs are ¾ inch apart. If it is uneven, equalize the legs of the link by putting it in the swage block and hitting the long end. Then scarf the end. Hold it flat and at a 45° angle to the step of the anvil. Strike successive blows on its end, as you move it to the left toward the horn. Turn the U over and do the other leg. Do not make the scarfs less than $1/16$-inch thick on the end or they will be too thin to hold a welding heat. Close the end by bringing the scarfs together. Bend the legs at an angle; do not try to round the corners yet. This will concentrate the heat at the scarfs, when you put the link in the fire to bring the ends to welding heat. It will also be easier for you to hammer the weld.

Bring the link to welding heat and close the weld on the face of the anvil. Strike several light blows on each side and then place the link on the horn of the anvil to finish the weld. If necessary take another heat and give the link its final shape on the horn of the anvil.

Prepare the second link and complete the weld. Make a third and loop the other two onto it. Then weld the third link. You can add successive links one by one as you make them, or make several groups of two or three and then weld them together.

Other Hooks

Make a welded slip hook or grab hook quickly by bending a length of steel double and forming an eye at the looped end. Weld the doubled

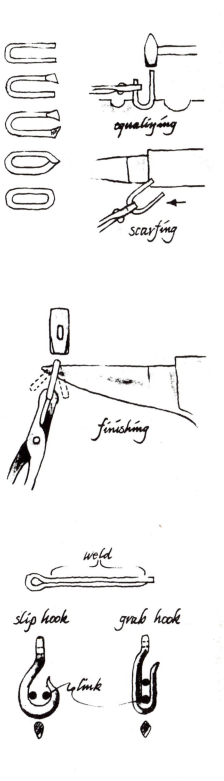

equalizing

scarfing

finishing

weld

slip hook

grab hook

link

portion and shape it into the hook. Because these hooks and the chain links are welded, it is best to anneal them after assembly to relieve the welding stresses.

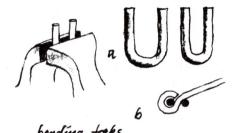

bending forks

Decorative Iron

Decorative or ornamental ironwork is generally assembled by means of bands, rivets or tenons. Gates, railings, signs and household accessories all fall into this category.

The tools that you will use to make decorative pieces should be made first. As with most blacksmithing tools, you will soon find many other uses for them at the forge.

There are two types of bending forks: those held in a vise and those placed in the hardie hole. The simplest ones are held in the vise; these are U-shaped forks (a). Select ½-inch and ⅜-inch round stock and make several forks of different sizes, varying the distance between the tines. (It is easy to bend an eyelet with a bending fork (b).)

Make the forks that will be used in the anvil either by gas or forge welding the U to a block that is similar to a small swage (c and d). Form the tines after you finish the welding.

Scroll or bending wrenches are handheld bending tools (e). Use them in scrolling, bending or straightening.

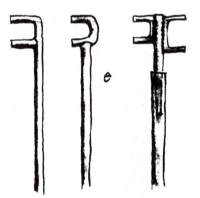

Scrolls

Scrolls are the filigree of the king's court. If your interests lie in the decorative area, the uses of scrolls are limitless. Although a scroll can be made free-form on the anvil, you will find that the scroll tool is a great help. Since scrolls are almost always used in multiples, the scroll tool will enable you to make uniform scrolls quickly.

To make a scroll tool, draw the outline of the curve and trace it onto a piece of sheet metal. When you are making the scroll tool the hot metal can be checked on this pattern. Flatten the end of a ¼-inch by ¾-inch bar and flair it up (a). (You will use this flaired end to start the scroll.) Then develop the curve to the pattern. Do this with a hammer over the horn of the anvil or use a bending fork and wrench. After you have made two complete revolutions in the development of the curve, bend the end of the tool at a right angle and double up the end to fit the hardie hole. Form the shank so that the scroll is about 1 inch off the face of the anvil.

Rectangular bars are generally used to make scrolls, although scrolls can also be made from round or square bars. To make the scroll, first finish the end of a ⅛-inch by ½-inch by 24-inch strap and start the scroll on the edge of the anvil or the scroll starter (a). Then heat at least 12 inches of the strap before bending the scroll. Place the end of the scroll on the raised tip of the scroll tool and grip them together with a pair of round-nose pliers. Then bend the strap in the direction of the curve. When one turn is complete, the scroll will drop completely into the tool. If enough of the bar is at a good heat, you can complete the bending in one heat. If the bar has cooled, return it to the fire and heat the portion to be bent.

Make the two basic scrolls, the C and the S in this tool. To make the S, turn the metal over to make a reverse curve. Make several scroll

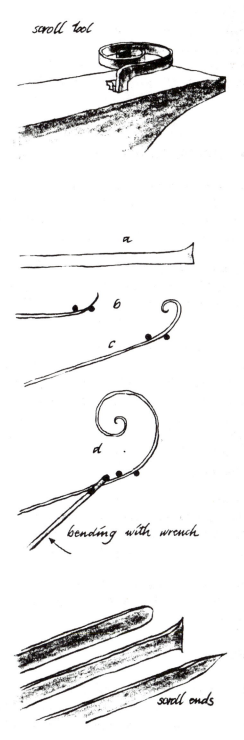

scroll tool

a

b

c

d

bending with wrench

scroll ends

tools to create different visual effects.

Trivet

Make a trivet to get the feel of making scrolls and assembling them. On a piece of paper, trace out a grouping of C scrolls to see how they would fit together. Then cut the stock into equal pieces and make the scrolls. To assemble the pieces, make enough collars or bands to join the scrolls together. (Allow an extra one for practice.) There are two basic types: a scarf collar and an overlap collar. It is easier to make a scarf collar, if you are working with thin strap metal, but when you are working with heavier pieces, then the overlap collar is better.

Scarf Collar

To make a scarf collar: Make a mandril by doubling over the stock that has been used to make the scrolls. Bend the collars around this, while the metal is hot. Determine the collar length by rolling the mandril over the stock used to make the collar. (This stock should be smaller than the stock for the scroll.) Using a chisel or hardie, make a diagonal cut partially through the metal, at the places you have marked off for each collar. Heat the bar and form the collar; then snap off the partially formed collar. Then complete the collar. While the collar is still hot, open it up with a pair of pliers, so that you can place it around the scrolls. After all the collars are formed, place several of them in the fire on a wire hook, or use a pair of pickup tongs with a coupler on the reins. In this way, they will not be lost in the coals. When they reach an orange heat, place the collar around the scroll. Close it with a small hammer; then use a pair of pliers to squeeze the scarfed ends together.

starting scrolls

on the anvil   on a scroll starter

a

b

Trivet

Overlap Collar

To determine the length of an overlap collar, add the circumference of the pieces to be joined to a figure which is 2½ times the thickness of the collar. Cut off a piece for one collar and draw each end to a thin taper. Then cold-form the collar into a U shape. Clamp it in a vise over a mandril made of the pieces to be joined. Make the first bend so that each leg of the U will be equal (f). Make the second bend around a mandril and a spacer (g). To install the collar, heat it and put it under the scrolls (h). Form the first leg over with angled blows. Then form the other leg over the first to overlap them. (A side blow tends to open up the collar, whereas the angled blow will tighten it.)

Welding Tips

Welding iron is a series of critical operations. It is not difficult, if you keep all of the elements under control. Make sure that you have scarfed the pieces properly, that the fire is a reducing fire, that you remove the piece from the fire at the proper time, that you have positioned the pieces properly and that you strike them quickly and surely.

Many people are completely befuddled by welding. However, when you have done each step carefully, and have "popped" a weld, you will feel more confident. Your first weld will be the hardest; as you learn and gain confidence from each successful weld, each one that you do will be easier.

Look at the iron in the fire. When you are welding mild steel, it is at a welding heat when the color of the metal and the color of the fire are one and the same, a light, bright yellow. In

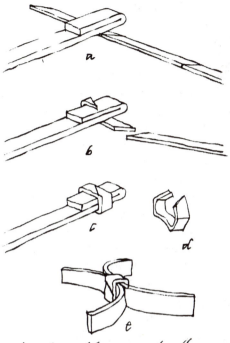

steps in making a scarf collar

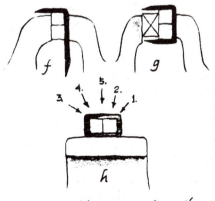

steps in making an overlap collar

contrast, tool steel at welding heat will be a shade darker than the color of the fire. Learn these things through experience.

There is another way to test for welding heat. Take a small rod, a ¼ inch in diameter, that has been drawn to a dull point. As the piece to be welded approaches welding heat, place the rod in the fire. Use the rod to check for welding heat. If the piece is at welding heat, it will be soft and the rod will stick to it. Try this test; it is very useful.

I have found that you must pay strict attention to your work when you are welding, perhaps more than at any other time. If you allow your thoughts to wander, you will burn the metal or miss the moment when welding heat has been reached. When welding heat has been reached, the metal will "speak" to you; it will give off sparks, saying, "Weld me."

Other Welds

To gain experience, let's try some different types of welds, such as the butt weld, the jump weld, T and angle welds and the cleft weld.

To make a butt weld, heat two bars of similar size to welding heat and butt them together by hammering the ends together. They upset one another as this is done (a). Finish the weld by hammering the sides; use a top and bottom swage to true up the shape. In general, use the butt weld on heavy pieces (¾ inch and over) and the lap weld (described earlier) for thinner sections of metal.

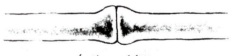

a butt weld

The jump weld joins a bar to a plate or another bar. This weld is sometimes used to make bottom swages and other anvil tools. Prepare

b jump weld

100

the two pieces to be joined; form a convex
scarf on one end of the bar and a concave scarf
at the center of the plate. When you weld these
together, the center of the convex scarf on the
bar must touch first to force out any scale, dirt
or flux that is present (b). This is critical. After
the stem is welded to the plate, turn it upside
down, put it in the hardie hole and hammer it in
to finish the weld.

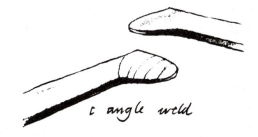

c angle weld

Scarfs for an angle weld are mirror images of
one another (c). Upset the ends and develop
the scarf, making sure that the edge is no
thinner than a $^1/_{16}$ inch; if it is, it will tend to
burn and to cool quickly. When you place the
pieces on the anvil to weld them, place them
together as you do when you are making a lap
weld, but at a right angle to one another.

Make the T weld in much the same way. Upset
the end of the T and the place in the bar where
it will be welded. Make each scarf face convex.
(When you upset pieces to be welded, make
them half again as thick as the original piece.)
When you make an angle or T weld, close the
weld with one or two blows. Quickly turn the
piece to work the other side. Then return it to
the fire and finish the weld.

d 'T' weld

Welding thin bands together is difficult because
they cool so quickly. Scarf the ends by splitting
and tapering the points; then interlock and
weld. Keep the split ends short.

With the cleft or V weld, you can weld spring
steel to mild steel; this is called steeling. (This
is used when the combination of tough steel
and hard steel are required, as for chisels, axes
and froes.) Form the lips of the cleft to wrap
around the end of the piece of spring steel. This
cleft grips and protects the spring steel in the

e scarf for thin bands

welding fire. (Use a flux containing 1 part sal ammoniac and 4 parts borax.) Remember, when you are welding steels with two different carbon contents, their welding heats are different. Place the mild steel in the fire to get maximum heat; push the spring steel through the fire to protect it. As the mild steel approaches welding heat, pull the cleft to the center of the fire for the final heat. Make the weld and finish off. Heat-treat it as necessary.

Crab Net Bow

Not all of you will want to catch blue crabs. But let's make a Crisfield-type crab net bow. This presents some interesting forging problems that you may encounter later as you are making other items.

First prepare the shank from a piece of spring steel that is 4 inches long and a ½ inch square. Draw out a taper and split the other end a ½ inch deep. Spread this end, and prepare the scarf as you would for a cleft weld.

Prepare the bow by drawing out the center of a 24-inch piece of ⅜-inch round spring steel. Make this ³/₁₆ inch in the center and taper it to ⅜ inch at the ends. The finished piece will be 40 inches long. Scarf the ends and then bend the steel into a circle and make a lap weld. Hold the bow with a pair of Vise Grips to keep the circle from rolling in your hand.

Place the shank over the lap weld on the bow. Close the lips around the circle at the weld, making sure that they grip it securely. Heat the circle, but not the shank when you are doing this, because this heats the inner part of the weld area, reducing the chance of burning the

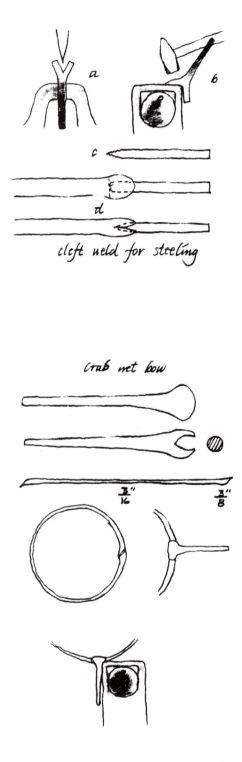

cleft weld for steeling

crab net bow

shank. Make the weld by closing it on the face of the anvil, then over the edge and the horn. Hammer-refine the weld area.

Make a special swage to help shape this type of weld. This tool would also be useful when you are doing multiple welds, when, for example, you are making a toothed tool, like a rake. The teeth of the rake are scarfed like the shank on the crab net bow and welded to a straight bar.

swage for finishing weld on crab net bow or rake teeth

Heat the entire bow to an even cherry red. Lay it down on the face of the anvil and straighten it with light taps. To make it circular, work it on a cone mandril, or on the horn of the anvil. Heat it to a cherry red and quench it in water to harden. Draw a temper to a light blue by using the flashing method on an open forge fire.

Upsetting a Ring

You may occasionally want to make a ring or hoop smaller. It may be a ring that has stretched, or it may be one that was too large to begin with. If you upset a portion of the ring, you decrease the circumference and, of course, the diameter.

Heat the ring and place it over a round bar on the anvil. Using a hammer, form a hump in that section of the ring. Heat it again and clamp it in a vise. Upset it by hammering. Then reform the ring into a circle. The area that has been upset will be thicker, but the ring will be smaller.

You have now come full circle by closing in on the basic processes used in forging iron. Use the techniques that you have just learned in new ways to gain experience and knowledge. Be creative. Forge ahead.

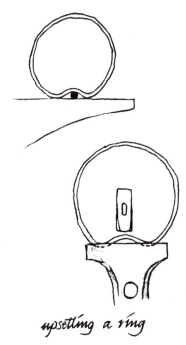

upsetting a ring

Section IV

Resource Information

Metallurgy for the Blacksmith

Metallurgy is the science and technology of metals and concerns the extraction of metals from their ores, the refining of metals, and the relationships between physical and mechanical properties of metals and their composition, mechanical working and heat treatment. Metallurgical information is helpful to any blacksmith, whether he is doing general blacksmithing or toolmaking. If you are a general blacksmith, then you need only understand the very basic principles; however, if you are a tool smith, then you will need a broader understanding. This does not mean that you will have to be a metallurgical engineer to make good tools, but that with some metallurgical knowledge, you will be able to select the proper material, forge it properly and heattreat it to develop the desired physical properties.

The basic forging processes are made possible because the iron becomes plastic and can be forged when it is heated to a cherry red and above, up to a light yellow. Iron can be welded when it is heated above this color range. When heated beyond the welding range, iron begins to melt and "burns"; this destroys the metal for forging purposes.

The structure of iron and all its alloys is crystalline. Plastic deformation of crystals is possible through the generation and motion of crystal defects called dislocations. These deformation processes operate with less deformation force as the temperature of the iron is increased. Thus, when iron is heated, it becomes more plastic. Generally, the higher the heat, the easier it is to form the metal.

A piece of iron is actually composed of many individual iron crystals, called grains, each having a different orientation of its crystal axes in relation to the neighboring grains. Normally, the size of the grains is too small to observed without the aid of a microscope. Sometimes, a fractured piece of iron will show evidence of the individual grains of iron that are visible to the unaided eye. The grain size is very important for determining the strength of iron: the more refined the grain size, the stronger the iron and the tougher (resistance to fracture on impact) it is.

There are two factors affecting the grain size that the smith can control at the forge: the temperature of the metal and the nature of the mechanical working (forging). The diagrams of grain size (a-c) illustrate what happens to the relative grain size of iron when is heated to a dark

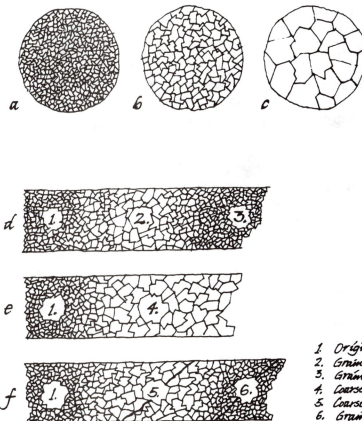

a   *b*   *c*

d   1.   2.   3.

e   1.   4.

f   1.   5.   6.

1. Original grain size.
2. Grain growth due to high temperature.
3. Grain reduced by mechanical working.
4. Coarse grain at welding heat.
5. Coarse grain at weld.
6. Grain hammer refined at weld.

cherry, an orange and a light yellow, then allowed to cool without any forging. It is easy to see that the higher the temperature, the larger the grain size.

When iron is heated and then forged, the forging refines, or makes the grain smaller (d). The forging must continue until the iron cools, below the critical temperature, to a cherry red. If the forging stops before the iron is cherry red, or the iron is reheated without further forging, the grain growth will resume.

Welding heat greatly increases the grain size (e). However, the weld can be hammer-refined (f) to break up the coarse grain. With this type of control at the forge, the smith doing general metal work can resolve most problems.

The toolmaker can use iron and mild steel for simple tools only. He must use special steels for tools that will be tough, hard and durable. To create these steels, alloying elements are added to the iron. The major alloy addition to iron is carbon. The chart of maximum attainable hardness shows the effect of increasing amounts of carbon in steel. Steels with only 30 to 40 points of carbon can be used where moderate hardness is required. (Steels begin to respond to heat treatment with around 35 points of carbon).

Hardness is the ability of a metal to withstand being deformed by indentation. This can be measured by a machine called the Rockwell hardness tester. (There are other tests; however, only the Rockwell C hardness scale will be referred to here.) A relative degree of hardness can also be determined by a file. (see File Test).

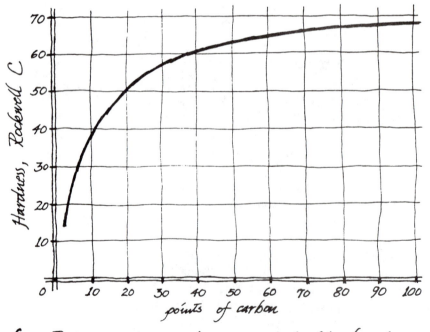

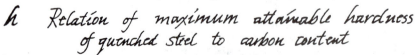

h Relation of maximum attainable hardness of quenched steel to carbon content

Chart (i) shows another relationship of carbon to iron: the differences of tempering temperatures on the hardness of three different steels, for equal tempering times. Notice that there is a greater difference of hardness between the steel with 35 points of carbon and the one with 80 points than there is between the steel with 80 points and the one with 120 points.

Toughness is the ability of a metal to absorb energy and deform plastically before fracture. The Izod impact machine measures toughness. Chart (j) shows the relationship between toughness and hardness as a function of tempering temperature. It is easy to see that there is a trade-off of toughness for hardness. Note the very steep curve as toughness increases to 30 foot-pounds.

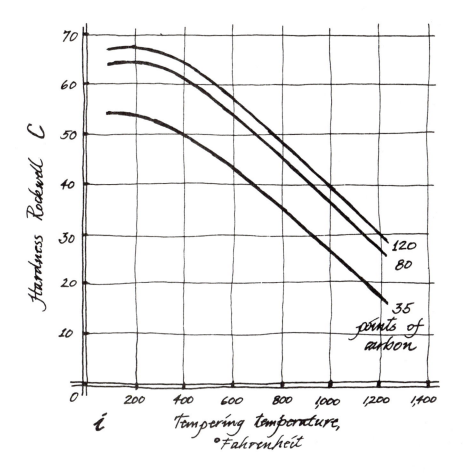

These are some of the observable properties of steel. What causes these to happen and what factors are used to make these changes?

The first test that you did when you made the center punch was to determine the temperature at which to quench the metal to harden it. This

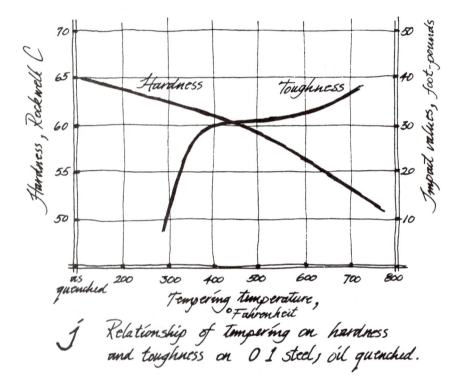

j Relationship of Tempering on hardness and toughness on O 1 steel, oil quenched.

temperature is called the critical point or critical temperature. What happens at this temperature?

On heating, the crystal structure of iron changes at the critical temperature from the body-centered cubic structure to the face-centered cubic structure (k). The face-centered cubic crystal has spaces between the iron atoms that can easily accommodate carbon atoms . Very little carbon can be accommodated in body-centered cubic iron. When an iron-carbon alloy is slowly cooled through the critical temperature, a carbon-rich "iron carbide" phase is precipitated; at the same time, new grains of the body-centered cubic iron are formed. However, if the alloy is cooled rapidly (quenched) the face-centered cubic structure trans

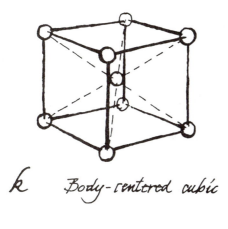

k   *Body-centered cubic*

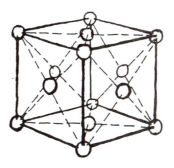

Face-centered cubic

forms to the body-centered cubic structure so rapidly that the carbon is trapped inside the body-centered cubic crystals. These crystals of metal are now in a highly stressed condition because they have cooled and changed shape and are supersaturated with carbon atoms (sort of a pregnant crystal). This makes the metal very hard and brittle. The degree of stress can be controlled by reheating the metal (tempering) and the desired physical properties of the steel can be tailored to the tool. Tempering also allows for the precipitation of submicroscopic metal carbide particles that strengthen and toughen the steel. Putting the steel in the stressed state is hardening; removing some of these stresses is tempering; removing all of the stresses is annealing. All of these processes are referred to as heat treating.

Another way of looking at this is to plot a temperature curve of iron (1). When iron is heated or cooled, the crystalline changes show up on the curve as steps or temperature arrests; these points are labeled A2, A1 and A4. Notice that at A2, not only does the crystal form change, but the metal loses its magnetism. The smith can use a magnet to determine the critical temperature for high carbon steels. He can place a magnet on the steel; it is at the critical temperature when the magnet no longer holds.

The major factor that influences the critical temperature of steel is the amount of carbon it contains. The phase diagram (m) is a chart that shows these relationships between carbon content, the ranges over which the different crystal structures are stable, and the various critical temperatures. The horizontal scale shows the amount of carbon in the alloy and the vertical scale shows the temperature. From chart (I) we know that point A_2 is the critical temperature (where the phase change occurs); on the phase diagram it is a line, intersecting with A_3 and then A_1, as the carbon content increases. Thus we can use this chart to de-

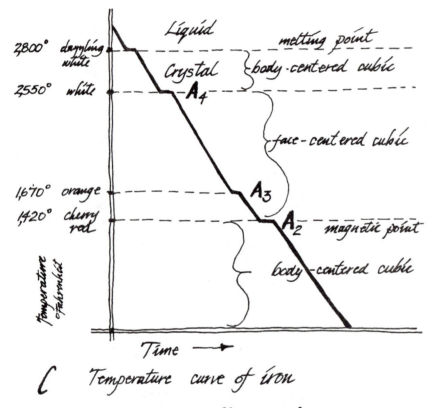

C Temperature curve of iron

termine the critical temperature of known steels.

The following temperature ranges may also be determined: for forging, for forge welding, for case hardening and for annealing and hardening.

With this background of information let us proceed to the practical aspects of toolmaking. As we have seen, there are three different steps in heat-treating steel: annealing, hardening and tempering.

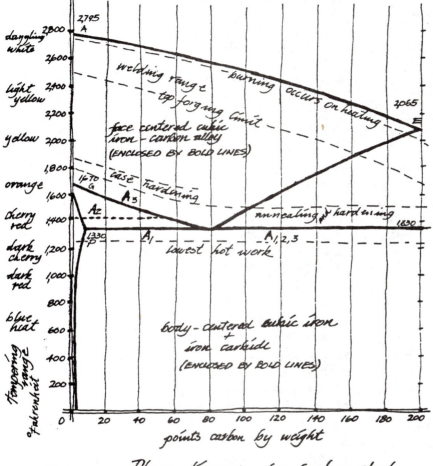

The simplest heat treatment is annealing, which is heating the metal to just above the critical temperature and holding it at that temperature to heat the metal uniformly, and then cooling it slowly in a dry medium, such as fine sand, ashes or lime. Annealing softens the material and relieves any internal stresses from forging. Annealling is sometimes necessary to sufficiently soften a piece for a cold shaping operation such as by machining. Generally, annealling temperatures are kept low so as to avoid excessive grain growth. Notice the area on the phase diagram, indicating the range of annealing and hardening.

Hardening is the process of heating the metal uniformly to a drop temperature slightly above the critical point (A3) and quenching (cooling) it rapidly in a suitable medium. When you are heating the steel to be hardened, you must have a reducing fire and must heat the piece uniformly; heat it slowly and turn the piece frequently to get a uniform heat. Do not take the metal too far above the critical point (no more than 50 degrees F. above) for it will only increase the the grain size and weaken it. When the critical point is reached throughout, quench the piece immediately. Quench on a rising heat, not a falling heat; in this way, you will not enlarge the grains excessively.

To harden steel, it is important to cool the metal quickly. Different media give different cooling rates. Those most frequently used are listed in the order, beginning with the fastest: 10-percent brine solution, cold water, warm water, cold oil, warm oil, air. Use the proper quenching medium for each steel. If you use a quench that cools the steel too rapidly, it will create excessive stresses and cracks will form. To avoid this, a slower quench medium should be used.

The mass of the piece is another important factor in the hardening process. A small thin piece, like a knife, will cool quite rapidly, but a heavier, thicker piece, like a hardie, will cool much more slowly, regardless of the quench medium, because the heat has to be drawn through the metal (the cooled part acts as an insulator). The rate at which a piece cools is important. It must cool quickly enough to harden properly. To offset the problems caused by slow cooling,any use a steel that contains alloying elements in addition to carbon. The desired physical properties will then be maintained. The ability of the iron to be hardened in depth consistently is hardenability. Hardenability is increased by the following alloying elements, listed in order of decreasing potency: manganese, molybdenum, chromium, silicon and nickel.

It is important to understand the difference between the maximum hardness obtainable in a steel and its hardenability. In plain carbon steels the hardness is a function of the carbon content only (e), whereas hardenability is concerned with the depth of hardening.

After a piece has been hardened, it should be tempered as soon as possible. A hardened piece is very highly stressed and can easily develop cracks if it is just laid aside. For the same reason, do not drop it, for it might break.

The temperature at which the temper is drawn is determined by the function of the piece and the desired qualities. The effect of tempering a fully hardened carbon steel is shown in (i), and it can easily be seen that as the temperature of the tempering increases, the hardness goes down. The result of this is shown in chart (j) which shows the trade-off of hardness for toughness. Understanding this relationship is very important for the blacksmith making tools. A cold chisel must be tough and yet remain sharp, a razor must be extremely hard to hold an edge and a spring must be flexible and durable.

The chart of temper colors gives oxidizing colors for a temperature and the tool for that range. This chart is a guide and it is advisable to test out your tempers for the tools you are making, because of the many variables that can change the results.

There are several methods for raising the temperature of steel to be tempered: a furnace, hot oil, gas torch and the forge. The furnace offers the greatest control, since it can be set up with temperature controls. Hot oil has limits, because it will catch on fire if it gets too hot, but its temperature can be controlled easily. The gas welding torch is particularly useful when you are tempering the sections of a piece differently, but it is very hot, so be careful. The forge is used for most tempering and with experience just about anything can be done at the forge. The limitation is the smith's ability to recognize the oxidizing colors and judge the temper temperature from that.

To temper flat springs, use a pot of melted saltpeter, or use a pan of fine sand to heat the piece and draw to the desired color. Linseed oil boils at 600°F: this is a good temperature for saws.

Another method for drawing a temper is called flashing. This is used to temper springs in the blue colors (around 600°F.), for oil flashes (catches on fire) at this heat. Dip the piece to be tempered in the oil and put it on top of the coals in the forge; move the piece around to get an even heat. When the oil flashes, quench the piece in the oil. Repeat this process several times to develop an even temper on the entire piece.

If you are making a tool that must be tough and strong, use a steel that contains one of the following alloying elements (listed in order of decreasing potency): titanium, vanadium, molybdenum, tungsten,

Expanded Temperature Chart
of Temper Colors

Color	°F	Use
	660	
Steel grey	650	
	640	
Greenish blue	630	Light springs
	620	
Light blue	610	Screwdrivers
	600	Wood saws, punches
Dark blue	590	Springs
	580	Picks, hot chisels
Blue	570	Cold chisels, light work
	560	Knives
Dark purple	550	Cold chisels, steel
Purple	540	Axes, center punch
Light purple	530	Hammers, sledges
Brown with purple spots	520	Surgical instruments
Dark brown	510	Twist drills
Bronze	500	Rock drills
Dark straw	490	Wood chisels
Golden straw	480	Drifts, leather dies
Straw	470	Pen knives
Straw yellow	460	Thread cutting tools
Yellow	450	Planer tools
Light yellow	440	Drills for stone
	430	Paper cutters, lathe tools
Pale yellow	420	Razors
	410	Burnishers
	400	Scrapers

chromium and manganese. These alloys refine the grain of the steel and give it the necessary toughness and strength.

Decarburization is the diffusion of the carbon in the steel to the surface, where it burns off in an oxidizing atmosphere. The surface of the metal loses carbon and some of its important alloying effects. This is no problem with mild steels, but is critical with tool steels. Therefore, it is important to keep the forge fire a reducing fire, and to use as few heats as possible. Steels vary in their rates of decarburization. The decarburized skin can be removed by machining operations. If you remove about .010 to .020 inch of the metal surface, this will clean off the decarburized metal. This is the normal amount required to dress most tools, knives or special parts.

Charts of Forging and Tempering Colors

The charts of forging and tempering colors are usually separated, but they have been combined here in an attempt to clarify this aspect for the beginning smith. The two ranges of colors should be learned. Experience is the best teacher, though.

The incandescent forging colors are created when iron is heated in the forge. However, describing any color verbally is impossible, partly because the colors change when viewed under different lighting conditions. Therefore, it is necessary to establish a constant. This will be cherry red, at the temperature of I ,420°F. (this is also the transformation point A2, shown on charts I and m above.)

It is easy to determine this temperature at the forge; when iron is heated and reaches this point, it becomes nonmagnetic. You can thus be assured of this point, regardless of the lighting conditions where you are working. This cherry red is the fixed unwavering point, against which all other temperatures and colors are relative.

The temper colors are created on the surface of a piece of polished iron when it is heated. The colors are a result of oxidation; as the temperature increases, the color becomes deeper. A rainbow of colors is created; these are indicated on an expanded chart along with the temperature and the type of tool that is to be tempered. Viewing conditions also affect these colors, although not as much as the forging colors.

Forging and Temper Colors

Color	°F.	°C.	Note
dazzling white		1,500	wrought iron burns
	2,700		
	2,600	1,400	top forging limit for wrought iron
white	2,500		
	2,400	1,300	
light yellow	2,300		
	2,200	1,200	
	2,100		
yellow	2,000	1,100	
	1,900		
orange	1,800	1,000	scale falls off freely
	1,700	900	
light cherry	1,600		scale forms & adheres
	1,500	800	
cherry red	1,400		
dark cherry	1,300	700	
blood red	1,200		lowest hot forging finishing heat
	1,100	600	
dark red	1,000		
	900	500	hardly visible in daylight
blue heat range	800	400	
	700		
light blue	600	300	oil flashes
dark blue	500		
brown	400	200	oil smokes
dark straw	300		
light yellow	200	100	water dries quickly
	100	0	

Forging Colors (incandescent)

Temper Colors (oxidizing)

However, there are several variables which do affect these colors: the manner in which the piece is polished or ground, the presence of any surface film of wax or oil, the shape and mass of the piece, the time it takes to heat it and the type of fire used to heat the piece. (Some fires or torches can cause a carbon film, creating a false reading.) Heat several varying pieces of metal; in this way you will be able to see the colors and the way in which they change.

118

Carburizing

Carburizing is the process by which carbon is absorbed into the surface of the metal by heating it above its critical temperature (A3) while it is in contact with carbonaceous materials. This is also referred to as case hardening, since the carbon penetrates only the outer layer of the metal. With proper heat treatment, a hard case is created, with a tough internal structure. This is useful on parts where wear-resistant surfaces and impact or shock resistance are both required. Carburizing can also be used to case harden the more forgeable mild steels after they are formed, or on steels where decarburization would be a problem. Mild steel with 10 to 25 points of carbon can be carburized successfully. Steels with a higher concentration of carbon become excessively brittle during this process. If this is not a factor, then use the higher carbon steels. There are special alloys for carburizing.

To carburize the finished metal, pack the pieces with the carbon materials in a steel box or pipe. Seal the container to prevent the carbon from burning off and use a box that is heavy enough to withstand the heat of a long fire in the forge or furnace. Pack the metal pieces evenly in the box with a uniform layer of carbon materials around them. This assures even heating and uniform carburizing. Usually a 1-inch space between the pieces is adequate.

The carburizing agents must be of a fine, even-granulated form, so that the carbon gases CO and CO_2 can move freely throughout the container and into contact with the metal. It is the carbon gases, not direct contact with the carbon, that allows the carbon to migrate into the steel.

Commercial carburizing compounds are available, but you may want to mix up your own. In general, the mixture can be reused. The rule of thumb is to mix I part new to 3 parts used. The carburizing agents are: wood, charcoal, animal bone charcoal, charred leather, barium carbonate, sodium carbonate, calcium carbonate and sodium chloride. (The carbonates increase the activity of carburizing.) There are many other carbon materials that will work and can be tried, but do not use any materials containing sulfur or phosphorus (use only charred bones). Charcoal will not be active in the carburizing process for long periods of time, so use bone-based materials in addition to the charcoal to sustain the carburizing process. Oil, tar or molasses are sometimes used as binders in the mixture.

Two basic mixtures to start with are:

Hardwood charcoal	50 %	Charred bone	75 %
Barium carbonate	20 %	Hardwood charcoal	15 %
Sodium carbonate	15 %	Barium carbonate	5 %
calcium carbonate	10 %	Oil binder	5 %

Place the container in the fire and bring it up to the critical temperature, turning the container so that it heats uniformly. You can place test wires through small holes in the container; these can be removed and checked for incandescent color temperature to determine when the interior comes up to the proper heat.

The depth of the carbon penetration is determined by two factors: time and temperature. As an example, on a piece of mild steel that is held at 1,600°F. for seven hours, the penetration will be 1/32 inch. As the temperature is raised in 50° steps, it takes one hour less for the same amount of penetration. Thus at 1,800°F. it takes only three hours for 1/32 inch of carbon penetration. (This would be about 85 points of carbon.) However, the higher temperatures will increase the grain size of the metal, so you must decide what factors to control.

If the piece being treated does not have to be shock resistant, then you can take it directly from the container and harden it by quenching it in water or oil. If maximum refinement is desired, then use these steps for a 1020 steel:

1. Carburize at 1,650°F. for time desired and allow to cool in box.
2. Remove and reheat to 1,550°F.; quench in water (refines core).
3. Reheat to 1,400°F.; quench in oil (refines case).
4. Can now be tempered at around 300°F.

Cyaniding is the use of cyanide-based chemicals to form a hard case; however, cyanides are very toxic and should be handled with extreme care. Use them only in a well-ventilated forge and smithy. Do not breathe the fumes. Wear gloves and a face mask. A little of some of the cyanide chemicals in a cut can cause illness-so be careful.

There are some commercial mixtures available that can be used. Sprinkle them directly on the hot iron and allow this to melt. Repeat this several times before quench-hardening the iron. This produces a very thin case and is called superficial case hardening.

A deeper case can be obtained by a process called liquid carburizing. The liquid is a melt of sodium chloride (3 parts) and sodium cyanide (1 part); use a heavy cast-iron container and make certain that there is no moisture on the piece when it is placed in the melt; it splatters. It is also important that the piece be free of scale so the carbon and nitrogen can penetrate the steel. (In cases using the salts and cyanides, nitrogen is also an element in the hardening process.)

Another mix is:

Calcium cyanamide	4 %
Calcium cyanide	43 %
Sodium chloride	33 %
Calcium oxide	15 %
Carbon	5 %

As with carburizing, the depth of penetration of carbon and nitrogen is a function of time and temperature, but liquid carburizing is faster. The time in the melted solution ranges from 10 minutes to several hours. On a 1020 steel, the case formed in a 10 minute immersion at 555°F is 0.005 inch; in 30 minutes, about 0.01 inch. The maximum that can be obtained with this process is about 0.020 inch.

After soaking the piece, quench-harden it in water. There will probably be a little of the chemicals carried over into the quench water, so put it aside, cover it and label it **Poison**. When you are using the liquid carburizing process, you can give the piece an interesting mottled effect if you quench it in a solution that has saltpeter in it (1 cup per gallon).

To repeat—the cyanides are dangerous poisons handle and use them with care.

Forging Non-Ferrous Metals

Copper and the alloys of brass and bronze can be forged hot or cold. Working the copper and copper alloys cold requires that they be annealed. Bring them to cherry red heat and immersing in water. This eliminates the effects of work hardening. Lead as an alloying element in brass causes it to crumble. However, the brasses can be heated to facilitate bending. Naval bronze is the best of the alloys to forge hot, the small percentage of tin gives it a good forging quality, but not the full working range of iron.

Aluminium can also be forged hot or cold, but when annealing it bring it up to a heat that causes a pine stick to burn when sliding it over the metal. This is also the indicates the temperature where it can be forged hot. The melting point of Aluminium is around 1200 F°. So, be careful when heating aluminium for it will not show you incandescent colors but just a puddle of melted metal.

Monel can be forged hot and it best worked around the higher range of temperatures, from a bright red up the a light orange. Monel is an alloy of nickel and copper (400 series, 60 Ni, 40 Cu) and has a good high temperature strength. It also has a great sensitivity to sulfur which causes it to crack or show check marks on the surface of the metal. Take great care to have sulfur free coal or use a gas furnace.

When forging any of the non-ferrous metals it is good to check with your materials supplier for the latest technical information.

Forging Stainless Steel

There are two basic types of stainless steel: the 400 series, which can be heat-treated and is magnetic, and the 300 series, which cannot be heat-treated and is nonmagnetic.

The 400 series stainless steels have forging characteristics similar to low-alloy steels, but require about 50 percent more force to form the metal. Above a yellow heat (2,000°F.), changes start to occur in this metal which reduce forgeability, so the metal should be heated to this general level for working. A few stainless steels are listed in order of decreasing forgeability along with recommended forging temperatures: 410—2,150°F., 420—2,200°F., 440 A—2,100°F. and 440 C—2,050°F. Heat-treat them in the normal way: anneal, harden by taking to an orange heat (1,750-1,850°F.), and temper to the desired degree of hardness (oil or air are normally used). Stainless steels that are heat-treatable are: 403, 414, 420, 440 A, 440 B and 440 C.

The 300 series stainless steels are more difficult to forge because more force is required to forge them, and because they work harden at higher temperatures. Several 300 series stainless steels that can be forged are: 304, 310, 316, 321 and 347. It is best to forge them at a yellow heat. Anneal them after forging by heating them to a yellow heat and air-cooling quickly.

Identification of Metals

Identification of metals can be done by several methods: by examining the color, weight, surface finish, magnetic properties, by means of a spark test and by looking at the specification numbers.

If you do not know the exact nature of a metal, the simplest way to identify it is to examine the color, weight and surface finish. As you gain experience, this will become easier. A test for magnetism will help you identify iron-based metals, particularly if they have been plated or painted. This test can also be used to sort out the 400 series of stainless steels, which are magnetic, from the 300 series, which are nonmagnetic.

You can use the spark test to sort out the general types of steel, to determine the approximate amount of carbon in steel and sometimes to pinpoint the general type of alloy steel. To make this test, grind the piece on the bench grinder, and observe the sparks. You should make this test under carefully controlled conditions: stand upright, making sure that your line of view is perpendicular to the stream of sparks; make sure that the lighting is constant; and make sure that you exert the same amount of pressure as you hold each piece against the grinding wheel. (If you increase the pressure against the wheel, the temperature of the spark stream will be raised, changing its appearance.) Look for: the color of the sparks, the length and amount of the stream, the streaks and the nature of the bursts or feathering. Try this test on some pieces of steel that are already identified (and labeled). Use these as control pieces as you learn this technique. It takes experience and practice. Refer to the drawings and notice that, as the carbon content is increased, the bursts increase and the stream shortens. This is because greater concentrations of carbon burn more rapidly. Also, as the carbon content is increased, the stream changes from a light yellow to a white yellow. In contrast, high-speed steel is more of an orange yellow.

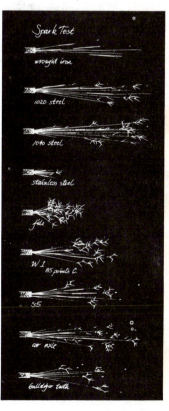

Specification numbers have been developed by the American Iron and Steel Institute, A.I.S.I., and the Society of Automotive Engineers, S.A.E., for all steels and their alloys (see chart). They are used when ordering or specifying steels. The specification number is made up of four digits: the first digit indicates the type of steel; the second digit indicates the percentage of the predominate

S.A.E. Specification Numbers

Type of Steel	Series Designation
Carbon steels	1XXX
Plain carbon	10XX
Free machining, resulfurized (screw stock)	11XX
Free machining, resulfurized, rephosphorized	12XX
Manganese steels	13XX
High-manganese carburizing steels	15XX
Nickel steels	2XXX
3.50 percent nickel	23XX
5.00 percent nickel	25XX
Nickel-chromium steels	3XXX
1.25 percent nickel, 0.06 percent chromium	31XX
1.75 percent nickel, 1.00 percent chromium	32XX
3.50 percent nickel, 1.50 percent chromium	33XX
Corrosion and heat-resisting steels	30XXX
Molybdenum steels	4XXX
Carbon-molybdenum	40XX
Chromium-molybdenum	41XX
Chromium-nickel-molybdenum	43XX
Nickel-molybdenum	46XX and 48XX
Chromium steels	5XXX
Low chromium	51XX
Medium chromium	52XXX
Corrosion and heat resisting	51XXX
Chromium-vanadium steels	6XXX
Chromium 1.0 percent	61XX
Nickel-chromium-molybdenum	86XX and 87XX
Manganese-silicon	92XX
Nickel-chromium-molybdenum	93XX
Manganese-nickel-chromium-molybdenum	94XX
Nickel-chromium-molybdenum	97XX
Nickel-chromium-molybdenum	98XX

alloying element in simple-alloy steels; and the last two digits indicate the average carbon content in points. For example, a 1020 carbon steel is a mild steel with 20 points of carbon; a 2325 steel is a nickel steel, containing approximately 3-percent nickel and 25 points carbon.

The specification numbers for tool steels are based on a letter prefix which describes the basic class of steel. A number following indicates the different types of steel in that class.

Tool Steels

High speed:
Tungsten base . . . . T
Molybdenum base . . . . M
Hot work:
Chromium base . . . . H 10–H 19
Tungsten base . . . . H 20–H 39
Molybdenum base . . . . H 40–H 59
Cold work:
High carbon, high chromium . . . . D
Medium alloy air hardening . . . . A
Oil hardening . . . . O
Shock resisting . . . . S
Mold steels . . . . P
Special purpose:
Low alloy L
Carbon tungsten . . . . F
Water hardening . . . . W

The type of steels used on General Motors
cars and trucks is as follows:

Leaf spring	5160
Coil spring	5160 or 9260
Axle shaft	1050
Transmission shaft	1141
Inlet engine valve	3140
Exhaust engine valve	ARMCO #21 - 4N
Connecting rod	1038 or 10374

Comparative Properties of Tool Steels

Type	Group	Quench Medium*	Wear Resistance	Toughness	Hardening Depth	Relative Cost	Resistance to Decarburization
M	high-speed	O, A, A	very high	low	deep	high	low-medium
T	high-speed	O, A, S,	very high	low	deep	highest	low-high
H	hot work: CR base	A, O	fair	good	deep	high	medium
	W base	A, O	fair to good	good	deep	high	medium
	Mo base	O, A, S	high	medium	deep	high	low-medium
D	cold work	A, O	best	poor	deep	medium high	medium
A	cold work	A	good	fair	deep	medium	medium-high
O	cold work	O	good	fair	medium	low	high
S	shock resisting	O, W	fair	best	medium	medium high	low-medium
P	mold steel	A, O, W	low to high	high	shallow	medium	high
L	special purpose low alloy	O, W	medium	medium to very high	medium	low	high
F	special purpose carbon-tungsten	W, B	low to very high	low to high	shallow	low	high
W	water-hardening	W, B	fair-good	good	shallow	lowest	highest

*W-Water,   B-Brine,   O-Oil,   A-Air,   S-Molten Salt

Carbon Content of Steel for Different Uses

Points Carbon	Properties	Uses
5-10	Very soft, plastic	Stampings, rivets, nails, wire, general forging
10-20	Tough	Structural steel, general use, good for case hardening, general forging
20-30	Quite tough	Better grade for structural and machine parts, screws, general forging
30-40	Very tough	Crane hooks, machine parts, connecting rods
40-50	Great toughness with little hardness	Heat-treated machine parts, gears, axles, shafts
50-60	Great toughness with some hardness	Crowbars, garden tools, gears, shafts, machine parts
60-70	Great toughness with fair hardness	Flatters, fullers, hot swages, tools to be used on hot work, drop-forging dies
70-80	Great toughness with medium hardness	All general blacksmith's tools, hammers, rivet sets, hot sets, wood augers, gun barrels, wood chisels, screwdrivers
80-90	Very tough, better than medium hardness with slight cutting edge	Cold chisels, hammers, sledges, hammer dies, shear blades, large springs, scissors
90-100	Fair toughness, hard with medium cutting edge	Pneumatic chisels, knives, punches, mills, reamers, taps, anvil faces, wrenches, railroad springs
100-110	Little toughness, hardness with good cutting edge	Drifts, swages, springs, stone drills, pliers
110-120	Great hardness with keen cutting edge	Planing tools, axes, saws, woodworking tools, threading discs, coil springs
120-130	Very keen cutting edge; somewhat brittle	Drills, taps, lathe tools, shear knives, basic steel used for cutting-tool purposes, files
130-140	Very hard keen cutting edge; brittle	Cold-trimming discs, razors, glass cutters, ball bearings, steel engraving
140-150	Extremely hard and very brittle	Brass cutting tools with fine edge, turning hard metals, tools used to cut other partially hardened metals

Finishes

Finishes must be applied to most iron-based alloys because they love to rust. I will describe how to prepare the surfaces and the various methods used to finish the metal, but first, in order to understand why iron must be finished, let's take a quick look at rust or corrosion.

All alloys of iron corrode to some degree depending on the alloy, the temperature and the environment. Iron exists in nature as iron oxide. After it has been refined into the iron metals that we use, it has a tendency to return to its more stable natural state, iron oxide or rust. This can be prevented (sometimes), that is, the basic electrochemical action of corrosion can be blocked. Corrosion is the flow of an electrical current on the metal when there is an electrolyte present; this causes oxidation. Thus when steel gets wet, a current flows, causing rust; if salt is added, the process is accelerated. Sometimes, as in the case of Cor-ten steel, a layer of rust will build up and block further corrosion.

In the case of stainless steel, a hard protective layer is formed on the surface, preventing further corrosion.

The simplest method that you can use to protect a piece of iron that you have forged, is to brush it briskly with a wire brush, to remove the loose scale, and then to rub it with oil or wax. When the iron is warm, the oil and wax can penetrate under the scale, forming a reasonably protective barrier. This type of finish may wear off with use, but it is easily replaced. Later you may want to rub the part with another type of oil. You can use peanut oil, linseed oil or machine oil. It is even better to use a combination of linseed oil and beeswax for most objects. To a pint of linseed oil that has been heated, gradually add a 3-to 4-cubic-inch lump of beeswax. Stir until the wax melts. After you apply this mixture to the iron, return the piece to the fire, so that the linseed oil will carburize slightly. Then apply another coating of oil and rub. Other mixtures of wax and oil may also be used. However, bear in mind that when you are treating objects that will be used in or around food, vegetable oils should be used.

There is another method for removing scale: quench the piece of hot iron in a brine solution, the steam created blasts the scale free. In addition, if you hammer-refine the piece as it is cooling, then the heavier deposits of scale will be worked off. However, if you want to make certain that all the scale is removed, you will have to use additional mechanical or chemical methods. You can use a wire wheel or any abrasive wheel; these wheels will polish the iron, as you get rid of the scale.

The method just described is alright for pieces that are simply shaped, and that have flat surfaces that are easily accessible. However, you may not be able to remove all of the scale on more intricate pieces, particularly in the crevices and corners. For those pieces, you must resort to chemical removal of the scale. The scale will be completely removed if you soak the piece in an acid "bath"; this is called pickling. Be careful not to leave the metal in the bath too long; if you do, it will pit. You must neutralize the iron with baking soda and wash it thoroughly after the pickle bath. Be extremely careful when you are mixing, handling and working with the pickle solutions.

Below are several pickle formulas. Hydrochloric acid works faster than sulfuric, but it costs more. Phosphoric acid does not leave a corrosive salt on the metal. These solutions work faster when heated.

1. Hydrochloric acid   1 gallon
   Water   1 gallon

2. Sulfuric acid   ½ pint
   Water   1 gallon

3. Sulfuric acid   6 ounces
   Ferric sulfate, anhydrous   5 ounces
   Water   1 gallon

4. Phosphoric acid   ½ to 1 pint
   Water   1 gallon

5. Sulfuric acid   8 fluid ounces
   Hydrochloric acid   10 fluid ounces
   Water   1 gallon

Resource Information

If you are going to use the piece of iron outside, then you should consider painting it to protect it. Make sure that the surface is clean; there should be no rust, scale, water, oil or grease. Prime the surface. A good primer is a must; apply a light coat, making sure that it completely covers the metal. Some good primers are:

1. Sherwin-Williams. Rust Control Primer #49, RED
2. Sapolin. Rus-trol All-Purpose Metal Primer #96, WHITE
3. Patterson-Sargent. Zinc Chromate Primer #49, YELLOW

Note that these are all colors which will show through if you do not cover them completely when you are putting on the final finishing coat, which is usually black. This factor will enable you to cover completely with the black coat, but do not apply it too thickly, or it will chip. There are many good finish paints, ranging from glossy to matte.

If any rust appears, clean the piece down to the bare metal, then prime and paint it. A spot of rust under the paint will continue to rust; it must be completely removed.

Al-chem makes a brush-on preparation for metal, which cleans it and prepares it for painting. It can be brushed on and then wiped clean. The preparation does not leave corrosive salts, as do the acid baths; instead, it leaves a phosphate coating that helps paint to adhere to the metal.

There is one disadvantage to painting the metal: the paint covers the natural texture and color of the iron. If you are going to use the piece inside, you can avoid this by painting it with a clear polyurethane varnish. This will give the metal a glossy satin or matte finish, depending on the varnish used. For variation, you can wire brush or highlight the iron with paint before varnishing it. If you want to highlight it with paint, clean it and then rub the crevasses and corners with a rag damp with black paint. Using another clean rag, rub off the paint on the highlights. Allow this to dry before sealing it with the clear polyurethane varnish.

Not long ago, as I read the *Fables of Aesop*, I came across the tale: "A Raven and a Swan." Perhaps it says something about how iron should be finished and how the surface should be treated.

Edge of the Anvil

Once a raven thought it would be great to be as white as a swan; he fancied that the swan's beauty was derived solely from its whiteness. He set about washing himself, he changed his diet and environment, and journeyed from his home to lakes and streams. But there the water was not good for him, the change of diet and environment took its toll and he wasted away and died.

The moral of the tale is this: Certain specific properties and characteristics should not be altered or changed. The raven failed when he tried to make himself white. Iron is not necessarily improved when its intrinsic beauty is covered up.

Blueing

We usually associate blueing and other coloring methods with gunsmithing. Most of the best information on blueing comes from gunsmiths. Some excellent sources which will give you the fine points about this process are: *Modern Gunsmithing* by Clyde Baker, *Metal Finishing Guidebook Directory* and *Phosphatizing and Black Oxide Coating of Ferrous Metals* by the Department of Defense.

These colors are created by means of the following processes: chemical solutions, which cause surface oxidation; chemical solutions, which change the surface of the iron into a different substance; and the combination of heat and chemicals, which cause oxidation.

You can use these processes on iron that has first been machined, polished, sandblasted or finished down to the bare metal. Clean it thoroughly to remove all oils and dirt. Any impurities will produce faulty coloration. First remove excess oils with a solvent and a clean rag. Immerse the piece for 5 to 15 minutes in boiling water, containing 1 to 2 tablespoons of lye per gallon of water. When it is clean, immediately immerse it in clear boiling water for several minutes. It will rust, if you do not do this quickly. Then, transfer it to the hot blueing solution, leaving it there until it reaches whatever color you desire. Use wires to suspend the pieces in the solution. Rinse it in boiling water, dry it and rub it with oil.

The blueing solution can be made up in different concentrations:

Sodium thiosulfate	3 ounces
Lead acetate	2 ounces
Water (boiling)	1 gallon

Another blueing solution is:

Ferric chloride	2 ounces
Mercuric nitrate	2 ounces
Hydrochloric acid	2 ounces
Alcohol	8 ounces
Water	8 ounces

Use this solution at room temperature. Clean the piece as previously described, and place it in the solution for 20 minutes. Remove it, and let it stand at room temperature overnight. Immerse it in the solution again for 20 minutes. Boil it in clean water for 1 hour. Dry it thoroughly; brush with a scratch brush and rub it with oil.

A third blueing solution is:

Water	1 gallon
Phosphoric acid	4 ounces
Soft iron filings	1¼ ounces

Clean the steel of oil and scale. Boil the piece for ½ hour in the solution; oil or wax.

You can impart a black or brown color to the iron if you use other chemicals and other, rather involved techniques. These techniques are described in the books previously mentioned.

An Old Recipe

Many of the old recipes refer to the chemicals that we use today in unfamiliar, perhaps ancient terminology. The following list covers the ones I have been able to find.

Edge of the Anvil

I question the value of the old recipes, although undoubtedly some of them are effective. The most elaborate recipe for a tempering compound that I have encountered is one that I found in a small book of 40 recipes by Capt. Daniel W. Young, *The Practical Blacksmith, Comprising the Latest and Most Valuable Receipts for the Iron and Steel Workers.* I have not mixed it up, but if anyone does, please let me know how it works and smells!

Take 100 ounces of yellow resin,

    50 ounces of cream of tartar,

    5 ounces of prussiate of potash,

    5 ounces of aloes,

    5 ounces of common salt; pulverize all fine together;

1,200 ounces of common resin, melted carefully,

    300 ounces of tallow (sheep tallow best); melt all;

    50 ounces of burnt ox claw or hoof (powdered),

    20 ounces of ivory black,

    20 ounces of saltpeter,

    10 ounces of sal ammoniac,

    5 ounces of powdered charcoal (live the best),

    5 ounces of gum arabic,

    5 ounces of alum,

    4 ounces of potash,

    3 ounces of burnt horn,

    10 ounces of cayenne pepper,

    10 ounces of chromate of potash, and add all the above to

    600 ounces of common fish oil.

Boil slowly and stir well for 1 hour; when cool it is ready for use. Superior for lathe tools, reamers, chisels, planers, mill picks, etc. With this composition you can attain excellent results if your steel tool is prepared or hammered with the application of no. 4 welding compound, then heated to a red heat and plunged into this compound, repeated three or four times, then tempered and cooled off in no. 6 fluid. It is excellent for edge tools and springs of any kind. This composition is of great value in any shop, and has been awarded three

133

first prizes at different European expositions. It is excellent for all cutting tools. as it avoids the warping and cracking in tempering.

Chemical Names

Acid of sugar	Oxalic acid
Aqua fortis	Nitric acid
Bichromate of potash	Potassium dichromate
Black oxide of manganese	Manganese dioxide
Blue vitriol Blue copperas	Copper sulfate
Borax	Sodium borate
Brimstone	Sulfur
Butter of zinc	Zinc chloride
Calomil	Mercurous chloride
Dragon's blood	Cannett root
Ferro prussiate Red prussiate of potash	Potassium ferricyanide
Green vitriol	Ferrous sulfate
Horn silver	Silver nitrate
Liver of sulfur	Potassium sulfide
Muratic acid Spirit of salt	Hydrochloric acid
Oil of vitriol	Sulfuric acid
Peach ash	Potassium carbonate
Sal ammoniac	Ammonium chloride
Saltpeter Nitre	Potassium nitrate
Water glass	Potassium silicate

Your Trademark

Your trademark should be applied to your work. It is your signature and has the obvious advantage of advertising you. You can use one of several methods: a special die made up by a diemaker; a simple one that you make yourself; a name stamped out with a standard set of letter dies; an acid etch on the piece.

DIAMOND FORGE

The dies are simple to hammer on soft steel. In contrast, if the piece is hardened, then you must sign it before it is heat-treated. Otherwise, use the acid. This is explained in *Modern Black-smithing* by J. G. Holmstrom.

To Write Your Name on Steel

Take of nitric acid 4 ounces; muriatic acid, ½ ounce. Mix together. Now cover the place you wish to write on with beeswax, the beeswax to be warm when applied. When it is cold, write your name with a sharp instrument. Be sure to write so that the steel is discernible in the name. Now apply the mixture with a feather, well filling each letter. Let the mixture remain about 5 minutes or more, according to the depth desired; then wash off the acid; water will stop the process of the same. When the wax is removed, the inscription is plain.

Other formulas for etching steel

1. Iodine   2 parts
   Potassium iodide   5 parts
   Water   40 parts

2. Nitric acid   60 parts
   Water   120 parts
   Alcohol   200 parts
   Copper nitrate   8 parts

3. Glacial acetic acid   4 parts
   Nitric acid   1 part
   Alcohol   1 part

Calculations

You must be prepared to make calculations in the following instances: to determine the weight of a piece, to determine the length of a piece to be bent and to determine the amount of stock required in drawing out, upsetting or other forging operations. A pocket calculator is a big help.

You can easily calculate the weight of a piece by multiplying the volume by the weight per cubic inch of the material used. Figure out the volume in cubic inches and multiply by 0.2936 for steel and 0.2779 for wrought iron. Refer to the charts containing weights for different stock.

When you are cutting off a piece of stock to be bent, remember that the centerline is the only part of the metal that will remain undisturbed. To determine the proper length to cut, use a traveler or measuring wheel. It is simple to use. With the pointer on "0," place the wheel at the beginning of the line to be measured. Push the wheel along the line, counting the revolutions as you go. Figure the length by totaling the revolutions and the remaining portion indicated on the scale.

An alternate method which is both quick and easy is as follows: Lay out a string or wire over the drawing or piece and then measure the wire or string.

When you are making a circle, use the centerline method. Multiply the diameter of the centerline of the circle by π (3.1416) to get the circumference. For example, in figure a, the centerline or mean diameter is 11.5 inches; the length of stock needed for the circle is 11.5 × π or 36.128 inches. (Note on the decimal equivalent chart that .128 is close to ⅛.) If you are going to weld the ring, allow about ¾ inch extra at each end, as each end must be upset to make the scarfs (½ inch for scarfs and ¼ inch for overlap). The length would be 36⅛ + 1½ = 37⅝ inches.

Edge of the Anvil

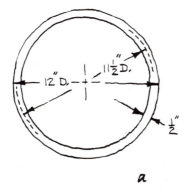

a

To calculate the amount of stock required to make the form in figure b, first calculate the length of each part needed to make up the piece. Then total the amounts. The piece is made up of three parts: A, B and C. A measures 1.5 inches by 1 inch on the face of the bar (cross section). Use that size bar. You will need 2 inches for A. (You do not need to calculate length since you are beginning with the proper size bar.) B contains 1.5 cubic inches of metal, and measures 1.5 square inches in cross section. To get the length needed for B, divide the volume (1.5 cubic inches) by the area on the face of the bar (1.5 square inches). 1.5 ÷ 1.5 = 1. Therefore you need a piece 1 inch long for B. Use the same method for C. C's volume is .75 cubic inch. Divide the volume (.75 cubic inch) by the face area (1.5 square inches) to get .5. One half inch is needed for C. Totaling these three amounts: 2 + 1 + .5 = 3.5.

You must also make allowance for loss incurred through sealing and the fillets in the corners.

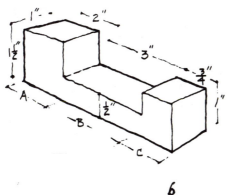

b

Inch/Millimeter Decimal Equivalents

Fraction	Decimal	Millimeters	Fraction	Decimal	Millimeters
1/64	.015625	0.39688	33/64	.515625	13.09690
1/32	.03125	0.79375	17/32	.53125	13.49378
3/64	.046875	1.19063	35/64	.546875	13.89065
1/16	.0625	1.58750	9/16	.5625	14.28753
5/64	.078125	1.98438	37/64	.578125	14.68440
3/32	.09375	2.38125	19/32	.59375	15.08128
7/64	.109375	2.77813	39/64	.609375	15.47816
1/8	.125	3.17501	5/8	.625	15.87503
9/64	.140625	3.57188	41/64	.640625	16.27191
5/32	.15625	3.96876	21/32	.65625	16.66878
11/64	.171875	4.36563	43/64	.671875	17.06566
3/16	.1875	4.76251	11/16	.6875	17.46253
13/64	.203125	5.15939	45/64	.703125	17.85941
7/32	.21875	5.55626	23/32	.71875	18.25629
15/64	.234375	5.95314	47/64	.734375	18.65316
1/4	.25	6.35001	3/4	.75	19.05004
17/64	.265625	6.74689	49/64	.765625	19.44691
9/32	.28125	7.14376	25/32	.78125	19.84379
19/64	.296875	7.54064	51/64	.796875	20.24067
5/16	.3125	7.93752	13/16	.8125	20.63754
21/64	.328125	8.33439	53/64	.828125	21.03442
11/32	.34375	8.73127	27/32	.84375	21.43129
23/64	.359375	9.12814	55/64	.859375	21.82817
3/8	.375	9.52502	7/8	.875	22.22504
25/64	.390625	9.92189	57/64	.890625	22.62192
13/32	.40625	10.31877	29/32	.90625	23.01880
27/64	.421875	10.71565	59/64	.921875	23.41567
7/16	.4375	11.11252	15/16	.9375	23.81255
29/64	.453125	11.50940	61/64	.953125	24.20942
15/32	.46875	11.90627	31/32	.96875	24.60630
31/64	.484375	12.30315	63/64	.984375	25.00318
1/2	.5	12.70003	1	1.	25.40005

Sizes of Numbered and Lettered Drills

No.	Size	No.	Size	No.	Size	Letter	Size
80	0.0135	53	0.0595	26	0.1470	A	0.2340
79	0.0145	52	0.0635	25	0.1495	B	0.2380
78	0.0160	51	0.0670	24	0.1520	C	0.2420
77	0.0180	50	0.0700	23	0.1540	D	0.2460
76	0.0200	49	0.0730	22	0.1570	E	0.2500
75	0.0210	48	0.0760	21	0.1590	F	0.2570
74	0.0225	47	0.0785	20	0.1610	G	0.2610
73	0.0240	46	0.0810	19	0.1660	H	0.2660
72	0.0250	45	0.0820	18	0.1695	I	0.2720
71	0.0260	44	0.0860	17	0.1730	J	0.2770
70	0.0280	43	0.0890	16	0.1770	K	0.2810
69	0.0292	42	0.0935	15	0.1800	L	0.2900
68	0.0310	41	0.0960	14	0.1820	M	0.2950
67	0.0320	40	0.0980	13	0.1850	N	0.3020
66	0.0330	39	0.0995	12	0.1890	O	0.3160
65	0.0350	38	0.1015	11	0.1910	P	0.3230
64	0.0360	37	0.1040	10	0.1935	Q	0.3320
63	0.0370	36	0.1065	9	0.1960	R	0.3390
62	0.0380	35	0.1100	8	0.1990	S	0.3480
61	0.0390	34	0.1110	7	0.2010	T	0.3580
60	0.0400	33	0.1130	6	0.2040	U	0.3680
59	0.0410	32	0.1160	5	0.2055	V	0.3770
58	0.0420	31	0.1200	4	0.2090	W	0.3860
57	0.0430	30	0.1285	3	0.2130	X	0.3970
56	0.0465	29	0.1360	2	0.2210	Y	0.4040
55	0.0520	28	0.1405	1	0.2280	Z	0.4130
54	0.0550	27	0.1440				

Dry ash stick rubbed on steel produces these effects at the temperature indicated.

660°F.	becomes sticky
680°F.	more greasy
700°F.	starts to slide
720°F.	slips easily and starts to smoke
735°F.	slips very easily, smoke and a few sparks
750°F.	more sparks
770°F.	lots of sparks
790°F.	starts to flame

This test is useful when heating up a metal in the blue heat range.

Rules Relative to the Circle

To Find Circumference:
Multiply diameter by   3.1416,
or divide   ``      ``   0.3183.

To Find Diameter:
Multiply circumference by   0.3183,
or divide   ``       ``   3.1416.

To Find Radius:
Multiply circumference by   0.15915,
or divide   ``       ``   6.28318.

To Find Side of an Inscribed Square:
Multiply diameter by   0.7071,
or multiply circumference by   0.2251,
`` divide       ``   ``   4.4428.

To Find Side of an Equal Square:
Multiply diameter by   0.8862,
or divide   ``       ``   1.284,
`` multiply circumference by   0.2821,
`` divide       ``   ``   3.545.

To Find the Area of a Circle:
Multiply circumference by ¼ of the diameter,
or multiply the square of diameter by   0.7854,
``    ``   ``    ``   `` circumference by   0.07958,
``    ``   ``    ``   `` ½ diameter    ``   3.1416.

Circumferences of Circles

In Inches

Diameter	Circumference	Diameter	Circumference	Diameter	Circumference
¼	.7854	12	37.69	24½	76.96
½	1.570	12½	39.27	25	78.54
¾	2.356	13	40.84	25½	80.10
1	3.141	13½	42.41	26	81.68
1½	4.712	14	43.98	26½	83.25
2	6.283	14½	45.55	27	84.82
2½	7.854	15	47.12	27½	86.39
3	9.424	15½	48.69	28	87.96
3½	10.99	16	50.26	28½	89.53
4	12.56	16½	51.83	29	91.10
4½	14.13	17	53.40	29½	92.67
5	15.70	17½	54.97	30	94.24
5½	17.27	18	56.54	30½	95.81
6	18.84	18½	58.11	31	97.38
6½	20.42	19	59.69	31½	98.96
7	21.99	19½	61.26	32	100.5
7½	23.56	20	62.83	32½	102.1
8	25.13	20½	64.40	33	103.6
8½	26.70	21	65.97	33½	105.2
9	28.27	21½	67.54	34	106.8
9½	29.84	22	69.11	34½	108.3
10	31.41	22½	70.68	35	109.9
10½	32.98	23	72.25	35½	111.5
11	34.55	23½	73.82	36	113.0
11½	36.12	24	75.39		

Weight of Mild Steel Bars

Size	ROUNDS SIZE		SQUARES SIZE		HEXAGONS SIZE		OCTAGONS SIZE	
	Per Ft.	Per In.	Per Ft.	Per In.	Per Ft.	Per In.	Per Ft.	Per In.
1/8	.042	.004	.053	.004	.046	.004	.044	.004
3/16	.094	.008	.120	.010	.104	.009	.099	.008
1/4	.167	.014	.213	.018	.184	.015	.176	.015
5/16	.261	.022	.332	.028	.288	.024	.275	.023
3/8	.376	.031	.478	.040	.414	.035	.396	.033
7/16	.511	.043	.651	.054	.564	.047	.539	.045
1/2	.668	.056	.850	.071	.737	.061	.704	.059
9/16	.845	.070	1.076	.090	.932	.078	.891	.074
5/8	1.040	.087	1.328	.111	1.150	.096	1.100	.092
11/16	1.260	.105	1.607	.134	1.393	.116	1.331	.111
3/4	1.500	.125	1.913	.159	1.658	.138	1.584	.132
13/16	1.760	.147	2.245	.187	1.944	.162	1.859	.155
7/8	2.040	.170	2.603	.217	2.256	.188	2.157	.180
15/16	2.350	.196	2.988	.249	2.588	.216	2.476	.206
1	2.670	.223	3.400	.283	2.944	.245	2.817	.235
1 1/16	3.010	.251	3.838	.320	3.324	.277	3.180	.265
1 1/8	3.380	.282	4.303	.359	3.727	.311	3.565	.297
1 3/16	3.770	.314	4.795	.400	4.152	.346	3.972	.331
1 1/4	4.170	.348	5.314	.443	4.601	.383	4.401	.367
1 5/16	4.600	.383	5.857	.488	5.072	.423	4.852	.404
1 3/8	5.050	.421	6.428	.536	5.567	.464	5.325	.444
1 7/16	5.517	.460	7.026	.586	6.085	.507	5.820	.485
1 1/2	6.010	.501	7.650	.638	6.625	.552	6.338	.528
1 9/16	6.519	.543	8.301	.692	7.189	.599	6.877	.573
1 5/8	7.050	.588	8.978	.748	7.775	.648	7.438	.620
1 11/16	7.604	.634	9.682	.807	8.385	.699	8.021	.668
1 3/4	8.180	.682	10.414	.868	9.018	.752	8.626	.719
1 13/16	8.773	.731	11.170	.931	9.673	.806	9.253	.771
1 7/8	9.390	.783	12.000	1.000	10.355	.863	9.902	.825
1 15/16	10.024	.835	12.763	1.064	11.053	.921	10.574	.881
2	10.700	.892	13.600	1.133	11.780	.982	11.267	.939
2 1/16	11.360	.947	14.463	1.205	12.528	1.044	11.982	.999
2 1/8	12.058	1.005	15.354	1.280	13.300	1.108	12.719	1.060
2 3/16	12.778	1.065	16.270	1.355	14.092	1.174	13.478	1.123
2 1/4	13.519	1.127	17.213	1.434	14.911	1.243	14.259	1.188
2 5/16	14.280	1.190	18.182	1.515	15.747	1.312	15.063	1.255
2 3/8	15.063	1.255	19.178	1.598	16.613	1.384	15.888	1.324
2 7/16	15.866	1.322	20.201	1.683	17.496	1.458	16.735	1.395
2 1/2	16.690	1.391	21.250	1.771	18.403	1.534	17.604	1.467

Weights of Square Edge Mild Steel Flats
Pounds per Linear Foot

Width, Inches	Thickness, Inches											
	1/16	1/8	3/16	1/4	5/16	3/8	7/16	1/2	5/8	3/4	7/8	1
1/4	.053	.106	.159	.213	.266	.319	.372	.425	.531	.638	.744	.850
1/2	.106	.213	.319	.425	.531	.638	.744	.850	1.063	1.275	1.488	1.700
3/4	.159	.319	.478	.638	.797	.956	1.116	1.275	1.594	1.913	2.231	2.550
1	.213	.425	.638	.850	1.063	1.275	1.488	1.700	2.125	2.550	2.975	3.400
1 1/4	.266	.531	.797	1.063	1.328	1.594	1.859	2.125	2.656	3.188	3.719	4.250
1 1/2	.319	.638	.956	1.275	1.594	1.913	2.231	2.550	3.188	3.825	4.463	5.100
1 3/4	.372	.744	1.116	1.488	1.859	2.231	2.603	2.975	3.719	4.463	5.206	5.950
2	.425	.850	1.275	1.700	2.125	2.550	2.975	3.400	4.250	5.100	5.950	6.800
2 1/4	.478	.956	1.434	1.913	2.391	2.869	3.347	3.825	4.781	5.738	6.694	7.650
2 1/2	.531	1.063	1.594	2.125	2.656	3.188	3.719	4.250	5.313	6.375	7.438	8.500
2 3/4	.584	1.169	1.753	2.338	2.922	3.506	4.091	4.675	5.844	7.013	8.181	9.350
3	.638	1.275	1.913	2.550	3.188	3.825	4.463	5.100	6.375	7.650	8.925	10.20
3 1/4	.691	1.381	2.072	2.763	3.453	4.144	4.834	5.525	6.906	8.288	9.669	11.05
3 1/2	.744	1.488	2.231	2.975	3.719	4.463	5.206	5.950	7.438	8.925	10.41	11.90
3 3/4	.797	1.594	2.391	3.188	3.984	4.781	5.578	6.375	7.969	9.563	11.16	12.75
4	.850	1.700	2.550	3.400	4.250	5.100	5.950	6.800	8.500	10.20	11.90	13.60
4 1/4	.903	1.806	2.709	3.613	4.516	5.419	6.322	7.225	9.031	10.84	12.64	14.45
4 1/2	.956	1.913	2.869	3.825	4.781	5.738	6.694	7.650	9.563	11.48	13.39	15.30
4 3/4	1.009	2.019	3.028	4.038	5.047	6.056	7.066	8.075	10.09	12.11	14.13	16.15
5	1.063	2.125	3.188	4.250	5.313	6.375	7.438	8.500	10.63	12.75	14.88	17.00

Coal

1 cubic foot of broken bituminous coal averages 49 pounds
1 cubic foot of loose bituminous coal averages 40 to 48 pounds
1 ton of bituminous coal equals 32 to 34 cubic feet

Weights and Melting Temperatures

	Pounds per Cubic Foot	Pounds per Cubic Inch	Melting Point in degrees F.
Wrought Iron	461 to 493	.267 to .285	± 2,790
Steel (1040)	489	.283	± 2,600
Cast Iron	450	.261	± 2,200
Copper (Rolled)	548	.317	± 1,980
Brass (Rolled)	542	.303	± 1,652 to 1,724
Aluminum	159	.092	± 1,218
Lead	711	.411	± 620

Blacksmithing Support Groups

There are several orginizations that support blacksmithing and metalwork: ABANA, BABA and NOMMA. The Artist Blacksmith's Association of North America, an organization of smiths, businesses and friends, is a major resource for blacksmiths. Membership is open to all. Their quarterly journal is an excellent magazine with articles, reviews, tips and resource information. Their address is: ABANA, PO RR5 Box 64, Nashville, IN, 47448. The British Artist Blacksmiths Association, composed mainly of smiths from Great Britian, is an excellent international resource for the metalworker. It also has a fine quarlterly journal. Their address is: BABA, Rosebank, Plaxtol, Sevenoaks, Kent, TN 15 0QL, England, UK. The National Ornamental and Miscellaneous Metals Association is more focused on the trade aspects of metals fabrication and forging. It has a journal that is published 6 times a year and covers a wide range of topics. Their address is: NOMMA, 804-10 Main St., Suite E, Forest Park, GA, 30050.

Each of these orginizations have regular meetings and shows that are always interesting and informative to attend. Usually there are demonstrations, lectures and dislpays of members work. A wonderful way to make friends and contacts.

Metric Equivalents
for Measures

1 inch (in.) = 2.54 cm
1 square inch (in.²) = 6.4516 cm²
1 cubic inch (in.³) = 16.3872 cm³
1 foot (ft) (12 in.) = 30.48 cm

1 square foot (ft²) = 929.03 cm²
                   = 0.0929 cm²

1 cubic foot (ft³) = 28,317 cm³
                  = 0.0283 m³

1 yard (yd) (3 ft) = 91.44 cm
                = 0.9144 m

1 square yard (yd²) = 0.8361 m²
1 cubic yard (yd³) = 0.7646 m³

1 mile (5,280 ft, or 1,760 yd) = 1,609.344 m
                                  = 1.6093 km

1 millimeter (mm) = 0.03937 in.
1 square mm (mm²) = 0.0015 in.²
1 centimeter (cm) (10 mm) = 0.3937 in.
1 square cm (cm²) = 0.1549 in.²
1 cubic cm (cm³) = 0.0610 in.³

                 = 39.37 in.
1 meter (m) (100 cm) = 3.2808 ft
                     = 1.0936 yd

                 = 10.7639 ft²
1 square meter (m²) = 1.196 yd²

                 = 35.314 ft³
1 cubic meter (m³) = 1.3079 yd³

                 = 3,280.83 ft
1 kilometer (km) (1,000 m) = 1,093.61 yd
                               = 0.6214 mile

Metric Equivalents
for Weights

1 ounce avoirdupois (oz) = 28.3495 gm
1 pound (lb) (16 oz) = 453.6 gm
1 lb per in. = 178.6 gm per cm
1 lb per in.² = 70.31 gm per cm²
1 lb per in.³ = 27.68 gm per cm³
1 lb per ft = 1.4882 kg per m
1 lb per ft² = 4.8824 kg per m²
1 lb per ft³ = 16.0184 kg per m³
1 net ton (NT) (2,000 lb) = 907.19 kg

1 gram (gm) = 0.0022 lb
1 gm per cm = 0.0056 lb per in.
1 gm per cm² = 0.0142 lb per in.²
1 gm per cm³ = 0.0361 lb per in.³
1 kilogram (kg) (1,000 gm) = 2.2046 lb
1 kg per m = 0.67197 lb per ft
1 kg per m² = 0.2048 lb per ft²
1 kg per m³ = 0.0624 lb per ft³
1 metric ton (1,000 kg) = 1.1023 NT

File Test

Action of File on the Metal	Approximate Rockwell C	Temperature	Temper Color
Hardened piece scratches glass	65	not drawn	
File slides off	60	400°F.	
File will hardly mark		420°F.	pale yellow
File can hardly be made to catch	58		
File marks		450°F.	straw yellow
File catches with difficulty	57		
File marks deeper		500°F.	deep straw
File scratches deeply	55	530°F.	light purple
		550°F.	dark purple
Files with great difficulty		570°F.	blue
Files with difficulty	53	600°F.	light blue
File cuts easier	50	660°F.	steel grey

Blacksmith's Beer

Blacksmith's beer is the name that my students at the Philadelphia College of Art have given my homemade beer. It is our custom to meet at my house at the end of each semester for a final evaluation or "crit." The students bring their work and I provide homemade bread and beer. At their insistence, I am including the recipe for my beer, which may prove to be a valuable resource for my fellow smiths. This idea was developed after several beers.

I dedicate this section to my students, who have taught me much.

Ingredients

10 pounds sugar
1 pound brown sugar
15 gallons water
2–3 pound cans "Blue Ribbon" dark malt
 extract, flavored with hops
2 lemons, juiced
5 vitamin C tablets
5 tablespoons salt
1 package lager beer yeast

Resource Information

I use a plastic garbage can with a lid, as my "mash tun," the container in which the beer, or "wort," works. (Please, use this only for beer brewing!) Mix the ingredients as follows:

Heat ½ gallon water in a large pot and add 5 pounds sugar. Stir until dissolved. Pour this into the mash tun. Repeat with the other sugars. Add malt extract and stir until mixed. Add all the other ingredients except the yeast. The yeast must be started or "proofed" by putting it in a cup of lukewarm water with a pinch of sugar. Set it aside until it has started (it will bubble up and "rise").

Make sure that the remaining water is warm, not hot, when you add it, so that temperature of the wort will be around 85°F. Now add the yeast. Place the cover on the can and let it set for about 2 to 3 weeks. The setting time is partly a function of temperature. Try to place the mash tun in a location where there are not too many temperature variations, and where the temperature will not drop lower than 65°F. Also, remember to place the mash tun up off the floor, so that you will be able to siphon off the beer into the bottles. The mash tun must be above the level of the bottles.

A beer hydrometer will indicate when the fermentation has stopped or "gone flat." However, any good smith can tell by color. Draw the temper of the wort to a "dark brown" that is clear with no bubbles rising to the top.

Using a plastic ⅜-inch tube as a siphon, draw off the beer into 1-quart sterile, returnable bottles. Fill them to within ½ inch of the top. Do not leave more air space, as too much pressure might develop. To get foam or a head on the beer, you must add sugar to the bottles before filling them. Add a level teaspoon of sugar to each 1-quart bottle (or ½ teaspoon to each 16-ounce bottle). This will cause a secondary fermentation. Cap each bottle and shake it twice when you place it in the case. Bottle caps and a capper are readily available in many stores.

Store in a dark cool space (or temper to a light straw).

In about 2 weeks, cool a bottle and see how it tastes. The beer should be clear and have a medium head. The beer really needs a full month to mature, but I cannot wait.

Cheers.

Bibliography

This bibliography is divided into three sections: blacksmithing, which covers the many aspects of forging processes, tools and materials; technical, which covers the metallurgical and scientific problems encountered in forging; general, which covers the historical and other aspects related to blacksmithing.

These books have been informative in my search and study of blacksmithing but they are only a partial answer. For, as the Chinese sage Lin Yu Tang said, "A wise man reads both books and life itself."

Blacksmithing

An expert blacksmith (Anon.). *Manual of Blacksmithing*. Chicago, IL: Gerlotte, 1902.

Anon. *Blacksmith Shop Practice*. Machinery Reference Series #61. New York, NY: Industrial Press, 1910.

Anon. *Forging Operations, Machine Forging, Forging Dies, Special Forging Operations*. Scranton, PA: International Text Book, 1916.

"Anvil's Ring," a quarterly publication of the Artist-Blacksmith Association of North America, 873 Spring Street, NW, Atlanta, GA 30308.

Bacon, John Lord. *Forge-Practice and the Heat Treatment of Steel*. New York, NY: Wiley & Sons, 1919.

————. *Forging*. Revised by Carl Johnson. Chicago, IL: American Technical Society, 1932.

Bealer, Alex W. *The Art of Blacksmithing*. rev. ed. New York, NY: Funk & Wagnalls, 1969.

Bollinger, J. W. *Elementary Wrought Iron*. Milwaukee, WI: Bruce, 1930.

Casterlin, Warren S. *Steel Working and Tool Dressing*. New York, NY: M. T. Richardson, 1914.

Resource Information

Cathcart, W. H. *The Value of Science in the Smithy and Forge.* London: C. Griffin, 1916.

Council for Small Industries in Rural Areas. *The Blacksmith's Craft: An Introduction to Smithing for Apprentices and Craftsmen.* London: Council for Small Industries in Rural Areas, 1952.

————. *Decorative Ironwork: Some Aspects of Design and Technique.* London: Council for Small Industries in Rural Areas, 1962.

————. *Wrought Ironwork: A Manual of Instruction for Craftsmen.* London: Council for Small Industries in Rural Areas, 1953.

Cran, James. *Machine Blacksmithing.* Machinery Reference Series #44. New York, NY: Industrial Press, 1909.

Crane, W. J. E. *The Smithy and the Forge: A Rudimentary Treatise.* London: Crosby Lockwood, 1885.

Crowe, Charles Philip. *Forgecraft.* Columbus, OH: R. G. Adams, 1913.

Drew, James M. *Blacksmithing.* Saint Paul, MN: Webb, 1935.

————. *Farm Blacksmithing: A Manual for Farmers and Agricultural Schools.* Saint Paul, MN: Webb, 1910.

Friese, John F. *Farm Blacksmithing.* Peoria, IL: Manual Arts Press, 1921.

Gooderty, Thomas F. *Practical Forging and Art Smithing.* Milwaukee, WI: Bruce, 1915.

Harcourt, Robert H. *Forge Practice: A Text Book for Technical and Vocational Schools*, rev. ed. Peoria, IL: Manual Arts Press, 1938.

Hasluck, Paul N. *Smith's Work.* London: Cassell & Co., 1899.

Holmstrom, J. G. E. *Drake's Modern Blacksmithing and Horseshoeing.* New York, NY: Drake, 1971.

————. *Modern Blacksmithing, Rational Horseshoeing and Wagon Making.* Chicago, IL: Frederick J. Drake, 1913. (This book is the same book as the preceding title which was republished under a different name.)

Horner, Joseph G. *Smithing and Forging*. London: Emmott, 1920.

Huges, Thomas P. *Principles of Forging and Heat Treatment of Steel*. Minneapolis, MN: Burgess-Roseberry, 1928.

Ilgen, William L. *Forge Work*. New York, NY: American Book, 1912.

International Library of Technology. *Machine Molding, Brass Foundry, Blacksmithing and Forging*. Scranton, PA: International Textbook, 1901.

Jernberg, John. *Forging*. Chicago, IL: American Technical Society, 1919.

Johnson, Carl G. *Forging Practice*. Chicago, IL: American Technical Society, 1940.

Johnson, S. S., and Warby, J. *Drop Forging Practice*. Philadelphia, PA: J. B. Lippincott, 1937.

Jones, Lynn C. *Forging and Smithing*. New York, NY: Century, 1924.

Jones, Mack M. *Shopwork on the Farm*. 2nd ed. New York, NY: McGraw-Hill, 1945.

Lillico, John W. *Blacksmith's Manual Illustrated*. London: Technical Press, 1930.

Littlefield, James D. *Notes for Forge Shop Practice: A Course for High Schools*. Springfield, MA: Taylor-Holden, 1910.

Lungwitz, A. *The Complete Guide to Blacksmithing, Horseshoeing, Carriage and Wagon Building and Painting*. Chicago, IL: M. A. Donohue, 1902.

Marquardt, Julius. *The Smith's Pocket Companion*. Duluth, MN: 1893.

Meyer, Franz Sales. *A Handbook of Art Smithing*. New York, NY: B. T. Batsford, 1896.

Miller, J. K., and Sekerka, John H. *Shop Equipment, Hand Forging, Tool Dressing*. Scranton, PA: International Textbook, 1940.

Moore, Thomas. *Handbook of Practical Smithing and Forging*. New York, NY: Spon & Chamberlain, 1906.

Resource Information

Moxon, Joseph. *Mechanical Exercises: or the Doctrine of Handy Works*. London: Rose & Crown, 1703.

Naujoks, Waldemar, and Fabel, Donald. *Forging Handbook*. Cleveland, OH: American Society of Metals, 1939.

Pehoski, Joe. *Blacksmithing for the Home Craftsman*. 3rd ed. Grand Island, NB: Joe Pehoski, 1973.

Richards, William Allyn. *Forging of Iron and Steel*. New York, NY: D. Van Nostrand, 1915.

Richardson, M. T. *Practical Blacksmithing*. 4 vols. New York, NY: M. T. Richardson, 1891.

Sallows, James Francis. *The Blacksmith Guide*. Brattleboro, VT: Technical Press, 1907.

Schwarzkopf, Ernst. *Plain and Ornamental Forging*. New York, NY: John Wiley, 1930.

Selvidge, R. W. and Allton, J. M. *Blacksmithing: A Manual for Use in School and Shop*. Peoria, IL: Manual Arts Press, 1925.

Smith, H. R. Bradley. *Blacksmith and Farriers Tools at the Shelburne Museum*. Shelburne, VT: Shelburne Museum, 1966.

Smith, Robert E. *Units in Forging and Welding*. Wichita, KS: McCormick-Matheurs, 1941.

Spons Mechanics. *A Handbook for Handicraftsmen and Amateurs*. 6th ed. New York, NY: Spon & Chamberlain, 1904.

War Office. *Handbook for Carpenters, Wheelwrights and Smiths*. London: His Majesty's Stationery Office, 1934.

Watson, Aldren A. *The Village Blacksmith*. New York, NY: Thomas Crowell, 1968.

Weygers, Alexander. *The Making of Tools*. New York, NY: Van Nostrand, Reinhold, 1973.

———. *The Modern Blacksmith*. New York, NY: Van Nostrand, Reinhold, 1974.

Wormald, Tom. *The Blacksmith's Pocket Book*. London: Scot, Greenwood & Son, 1921.

Technical

Althouse, A.; Turnquist, C.; and Bowditch, W. *Modern Welding*. Homewood, IL: Goodhart-Willcox, 1967.

Anon. *Metal Finishing Guidebook Directory*. Hackensack, NJ: Metals and Plastics, 1975.

Aston, James, and Story, Edward B. *Wrought Iron, Its Manufacture, Characteristics and Applications*. Pittsburgh, PA: A. M. Byers, 1939.

Bethlehem Steel. *Modern Steels and Their Properties*. 7th ed. Bethlehem, PA: Bethlehem Steel Corp., 1972.

Department of Defense. *Phosphatizing and Black Oxide Coating of Ferrous Metals*. Washington, DC: Department of Defense, 1957.

Digges, Thomas G.; Rosenburg, S.; and Geil, G. *Heat Treatment and Properties of Iron and Steel*. National Bureau of Standards Monograph #88. Washington, DC: U. S. Government Printing Office, 1966.

Handbook Committee, American Society for Metals. *Metals Handbook*. 8th ed., *Forging and Casting*, vol. 5. Cleveland, OH: American Society for Metals, 1970.

Hoyt, Samuel L. *Metal Data*. New York, NY: Reinhold, 1952.

Sabroff, A.; Boulger, F.; and Henning, H. *Forging Materials and Practices*. New York, NY: Reinhold, 1960.

Smith, Cyril S. *A History of Metallography*. Chicago, IL: University of Chicago, 1960.

United States Steel. *The Making, Shaping and Treating of Steel*. 7th ed. Pittsburgh, PA: United States Steel, 1957.

Watson, John. *Tables for the Use of Blacksmiths and Forgers*. London: Longmans & Green, 1906.

Westover, Ozro A. *The Scientific Steel Worker*. Wheeling, WV: Wheeling News, 1903.

Resource Information

General

Baker, Clyde. *Modern Gunsmithing*. Georgetown, DC: Small Arms Technical, 1933.

Baumback, C. M.; Lawyer, K.; and Kelly, P. C. *How to Organize and Operate a Small Business*. 5th ed. Englewood, NJ: Prentice-Hall, Inc. 1973.

D'Allemagne, Henry René. *Decorative Antique Ironware, a Pictorial Treasury*. New York, NY: Dover, 1968.

Davis, Myra Tolmach. *Sketches in Iron; Samuel Yellin*. Washington, DC: George Washington, 1971.

Encyclopaedia Britannica. "Iron." vol. 15, pp. 645. "Iron and Steel." vol. 15, pp. 649. "Iron in Art." vol. 15, pp. 674. "Steels, Alloy." vol. 21, pp. 368., 1955.

Ffoulkes, Charles. *Decorative Ironwork, from XIth to the XVIIth Century*. London: Methuren, 1913.

Gardner, J. Starkie. *English Ironwork of the XVII and XVIII Centuries*. London: B. T. Batsford, 1911.

————. *Ironwork, from the Earliest Times to the End of the 18th Century*. vol. I, II, & III. London: Victoria & Albert Museum.

Geerlings, Gerald K. *Wrought Iron in Architecture*. 2nd ed. New York, NY: Bonanza, 1957.

Gunnion, Vernon S., and Hopf, Carrol J., eds. *The Blacksmith, Artisan within the Early Community*. Harrisburg, PA: Pennsylvania Historical and Museum Commission, 1972.

Hiscox, Gardner D., and Sloane, T. O'Connor. *Fortunes in Formulas for the Home, Farm and Workshop*. New York, NY: Books, Inc., 1937.

Hoever, Otto. *An Encyclopaedia of Ironwork*. New York, NY: E. Weyhe, 1927.

Hughes, B. R., and Lewis, Jack. *The Gun Digest Book of Knives*. Chicago, IL: Follett, 1973.

Latham, Sid. *Knives and Knifemaking*. New York, NY: Collier, 1973.

Kauffman, Henry J. *Early American Ironware, Cast and Wrought*. Rutland, VT: Tuttle, 1966.

Mercer, Henry C. *Ancient Carpenter's Tools*. Doylestown, PA: Bucks County Historical Society, 1929.

Namuth, Hans, and Davidson, Marchal, B. *Early American Tools*. Verona, Italy: Olivetti, 1975.

Pennsylvania Farm Museum of Landis Valley. *The Blacksmith: An Exhibition of His Work*. Harrisburg, PA: Pennsylvania Historical & Museum Commission, 1972.

Schumacher, E. F. *Small Is Beautiful*. New York, NY: Harper Colophon, 1973.

Sloane, Eric. *A Museum of Early American Tools*. New York, NY: Ballantine, 1964.

Smith, Elmer L. *Early Tools and Equipment*. Lebanon, NJ: Applied Arts, 1973.

Sonn, Albert H. *Early American Wrought Iron*. 3 vols. New York, NY: Charles Scribner's Sons, 1928.

University Museum and Art Galleries. *Iron, Solid Wrought/U.S.A.* Carbondale, IL: Southern Illinois University, 1976.

University of Saint Thomas Art Department. *Made of Iron*. (catalogue) Houston, TX: University of Saint Thomas Art Department, 1966.

Wallace, Philip B. *Colonial Iron Work in Old Philadelphia*. New York, NY: Architectural Books, 1930.

Webber, Ronald. *The Village Blacksmith*. NJ: Pierce, 1971.

Wertime, Theodore A. *The Coming of the Age of Steel*. Chicago, IL: University of Chicago, 1962.

Wettlaufer, George, and Nancy. *The Craftsman Survival Manual*. Englewood Cliffs, NJ: Prentice-Hall, 1974.

Williamson, Graham Scott. *The American Craftsman*. New York, NY: Crown, 1940.

Young, Daniel W. *The Practical Blacksmith, Comprising the Latest and Most Valuable Receipts for the Iron and Steel Worker*. Dayton, OH: U. B. Publishing, 1896.

Zimell, Umberto, and Vergerio, Giovanni. *Decorative Ironwork*. London: Paul Hamlyn, 1966.

Section V

The Yellin Portfolio

The Yellin Portfolio

Samuel Yellin was born in Mogilev-Podolski, Russia, in 1885. After completing his apprenticeship to an ornamental ironworker there, he moved to Philadelphia, Pennsylvania, to join his mother and two sisters. He enrolled in the School of Industrial Art of the Pennsylvania Museum in Philadelphia (now the Philadelphia College of Art), and because of his experience and knowledge, was made the instructor of the classes in metal, which he taught for several years.

In 1922 he started his own forge, and gradually built up this business until there were 300 people employed. He was largely responsible for the revival of decorative ironwork in the twenties and thirties, until his death in 1940.

This chapter contains photographs of the ironwork of Samuel Yellin. They are small test pieces that he forged at the Yellin Metalworks in West Philadelphia. They are in a small museum there. Harvey Yellin, his son, still operates the shop. Because of their importance, these pieces, as well as Mr. Yellin's photographs, drawings, and library, are being assembled and will be housed in an appropriate museum in Philadelphia.

Samuel Yellin made these pieces in order to check out the ideas, thoughts and drawings that flowed from his creative mind. As his son Harvey said, "He used to draw ideas far into the night and always kept a pencil and pad on a table beside his bed so that he could put them down and not forget them." He describes how he felt about drawing and making these samples in an article he wrote for the *Encyclopedia Britannica*, the 1955 edition, vol. 12, called "Iron in Art."

> *Execution of Work*—First draw a sketch to a small scale, so as to obtain the general composition, proportion, silhouette and harmoney with the design of surrounding materials or conditions. This sketch should then be developed into full size to obtain details of ornament, various sections and sizes of material and a general idea of the method of making. At this time, careful consideration must be given to the practical use of the piece of work so that it may serve its purpose in the best manner possible. Workers in iron should always attempt to make everything direct from a drawing, rather than from models. When working from a model, the object becomes more or less a reproduction, whereas the drawings allow a greater opportunity to express the craftsman's individuality.

Studies or experiments in the actual material are now made, for here many things are revealed which could not possibly be shown on paper. The character of a twisted member or the flexibility of the material might be used for example to show how difficult it would be to conceive many things in the drawings. For this reason the true craftsman should often make a fragment or portion of the ornament in the actual material first, and make the drawings later.

The full-size pieces that he forged are located throughout the country. These are the magnificent creations of a master smith and bear witness to his genius. However, in this book, we will concentrate on his beginnings. The photographs of Yellin's work are included here to suggest possibilities and to challenge you. I hope that after you study them, you will be inspired to use some of the techniques or processes which Yellin used. As Yellin once said, "Where one possesses the ability, he can produce work in iron with a spontaneity that cannot be obtained in any other way." Notice that some of the pieces are assemblies of simple components; these show how larger grills or gates could be made. Study these things carefully and learn from them.

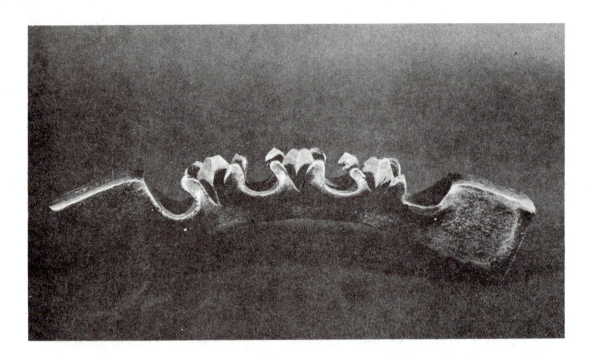

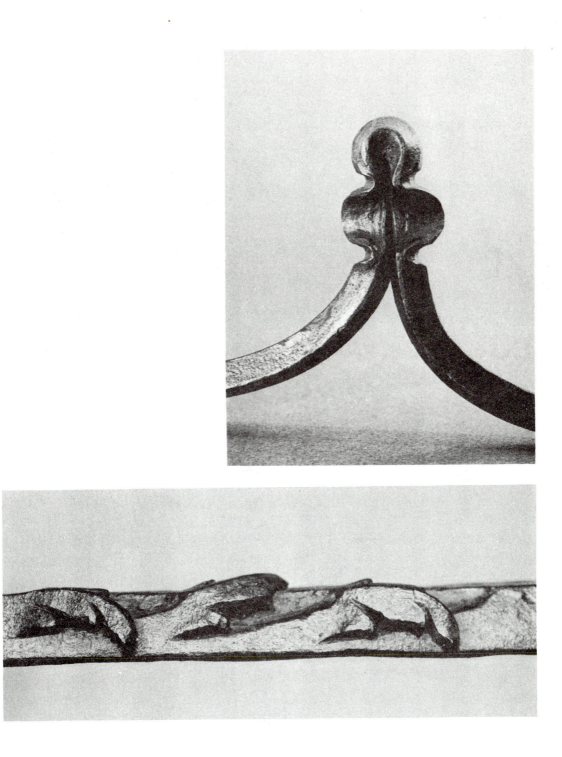

160

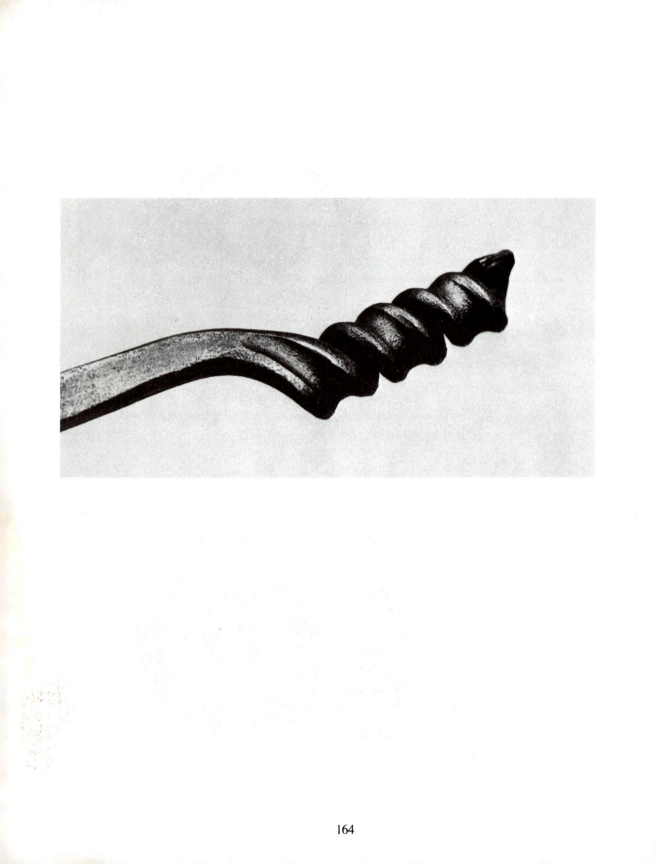

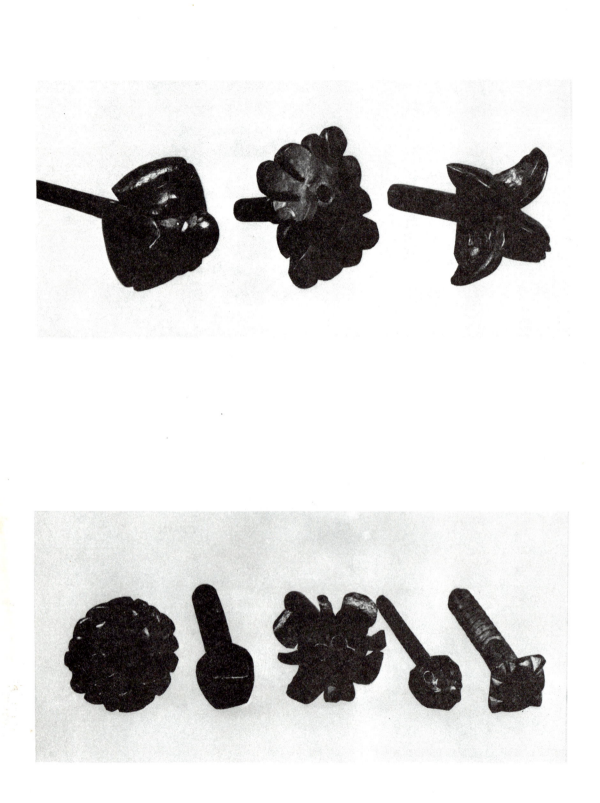

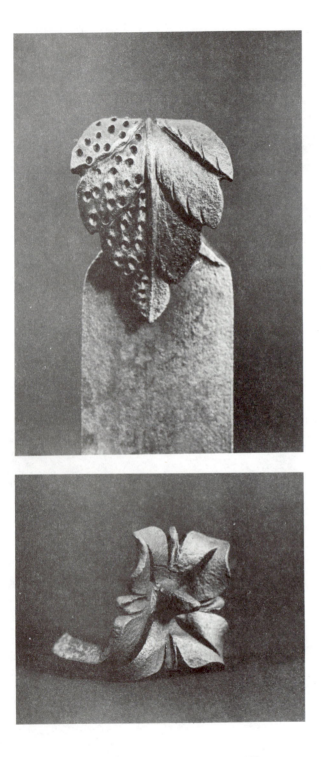

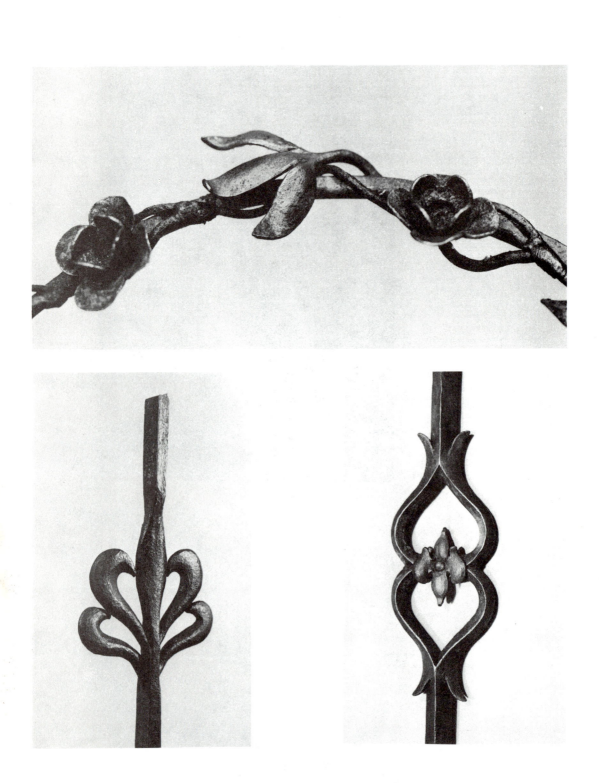

171

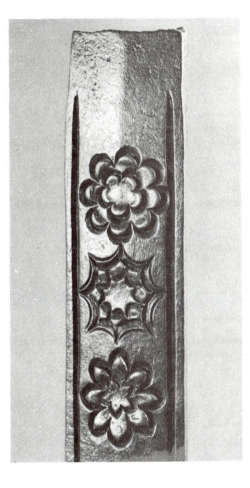

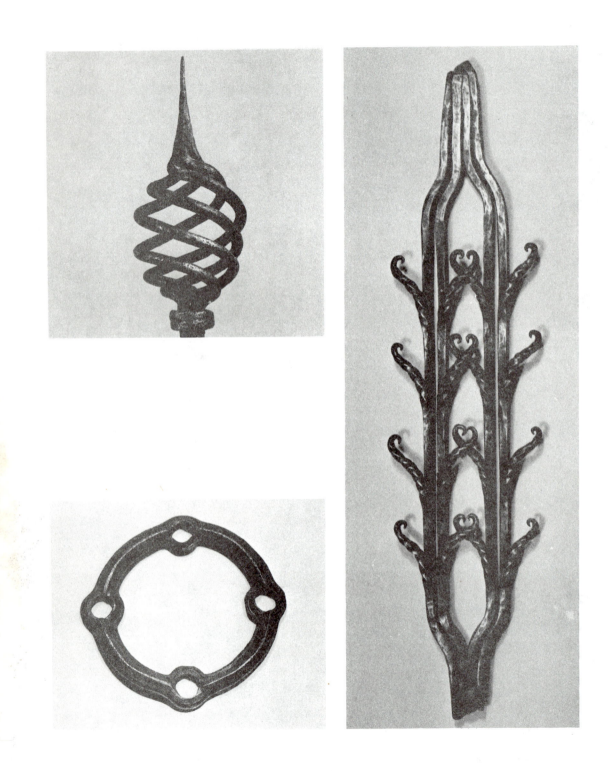

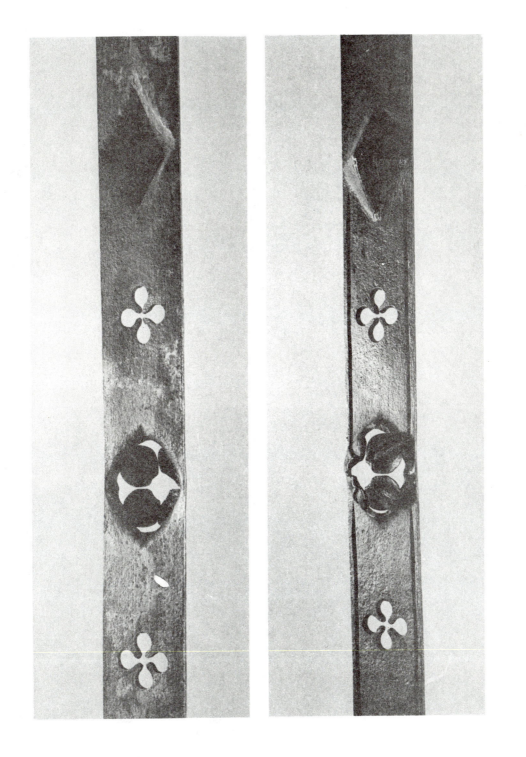

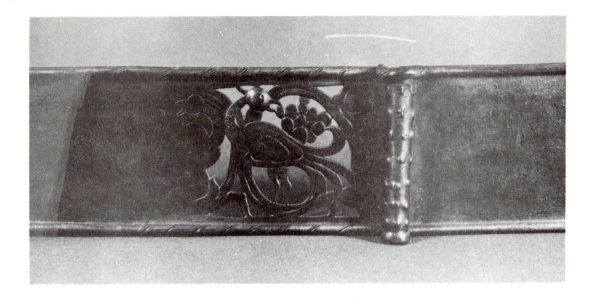

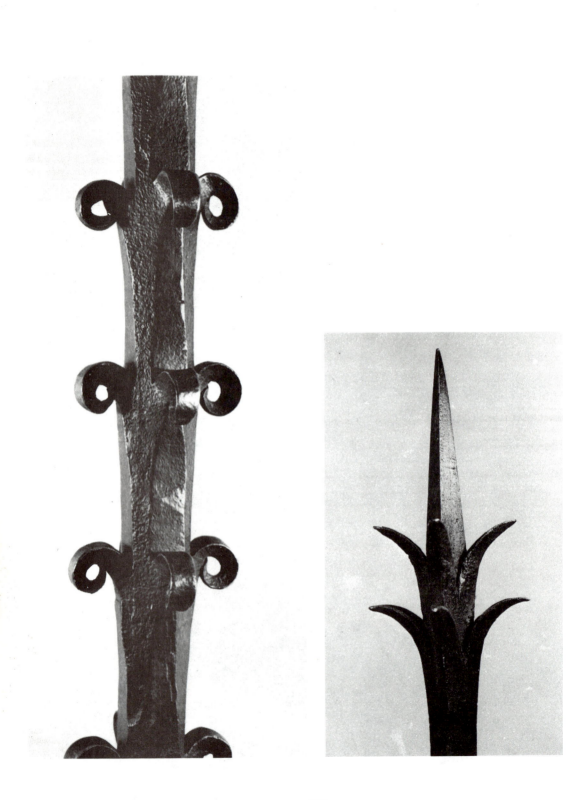

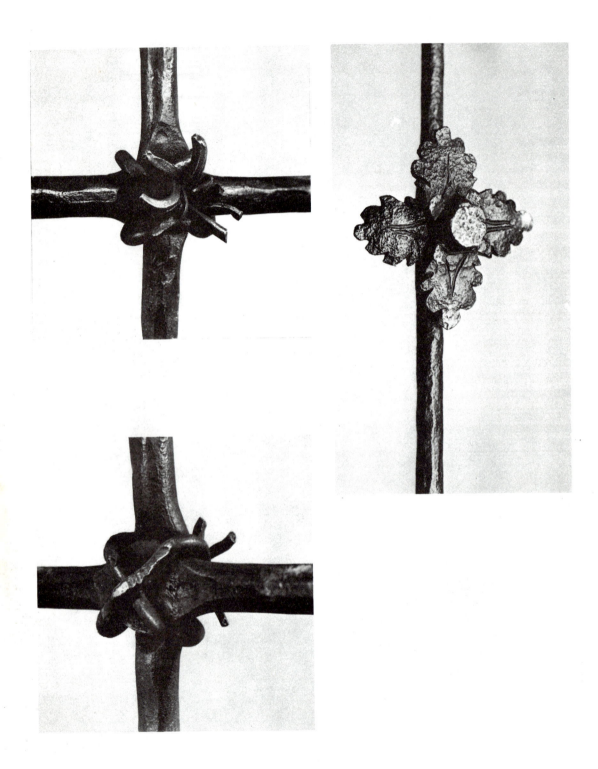

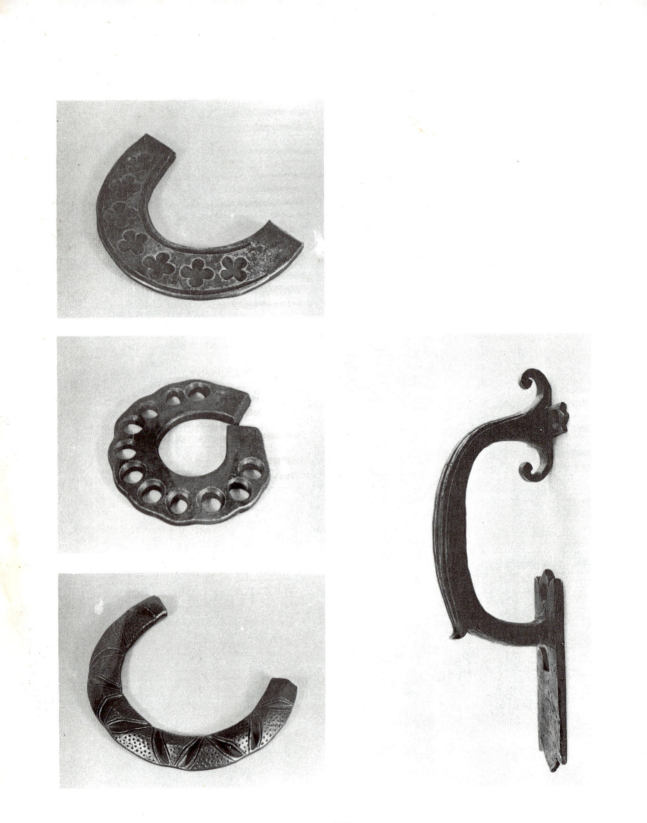

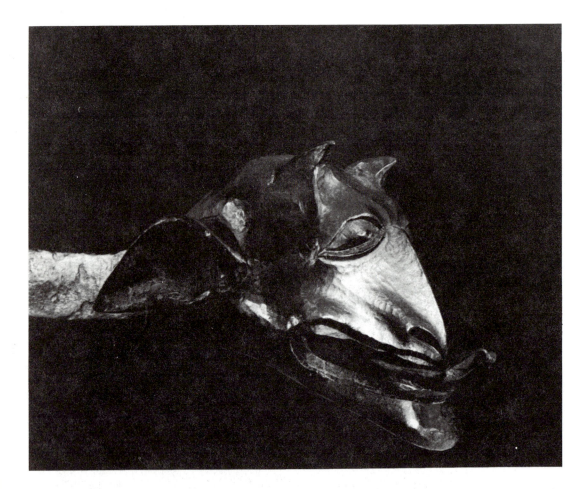

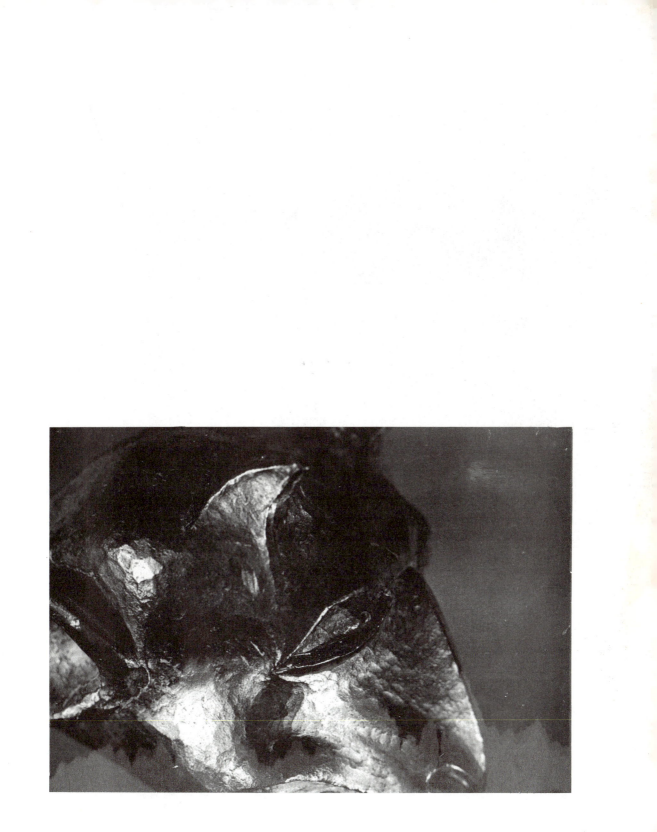

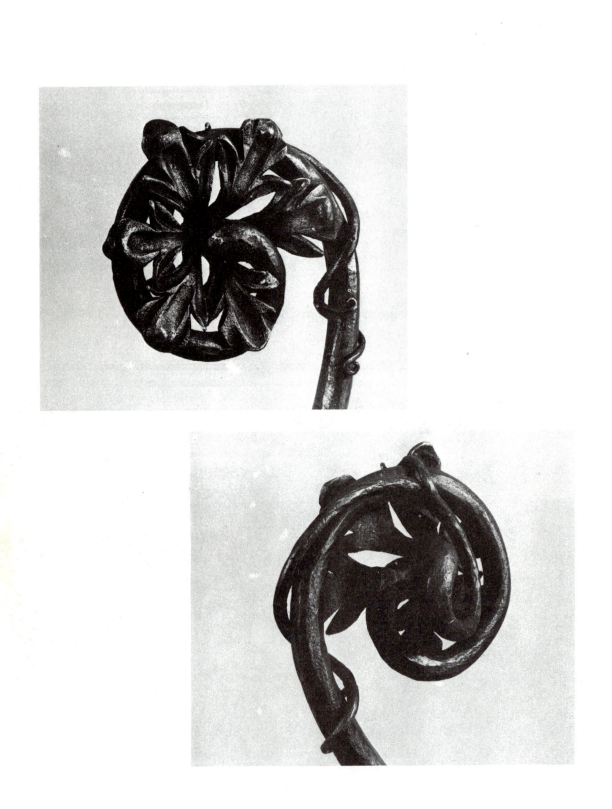

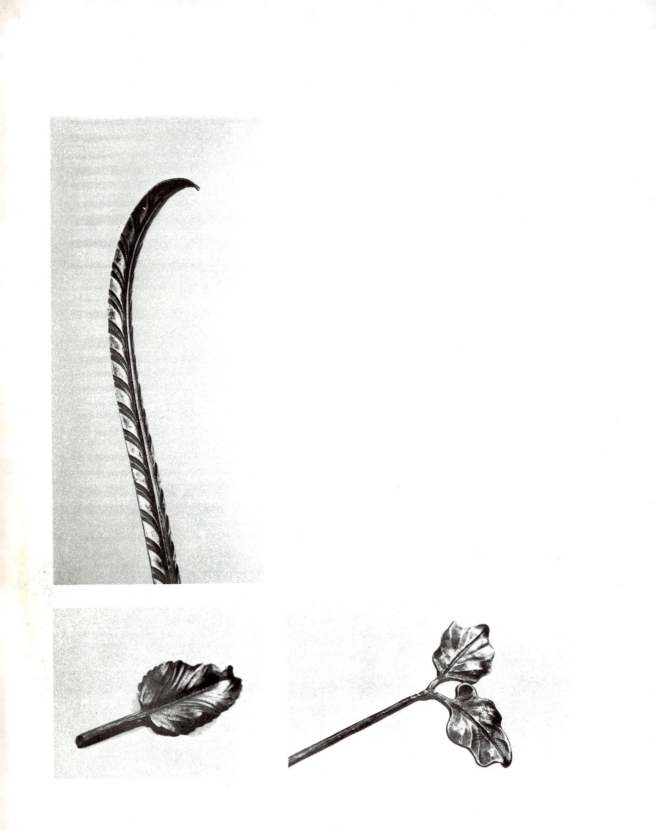

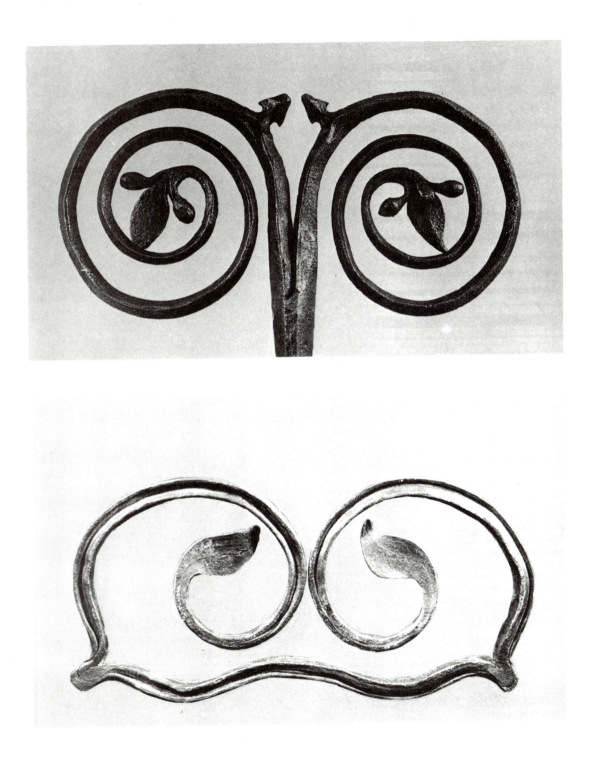

Postscript

The Ash Dump or "Zen and the Art of Throwing Pebbles"

When I started thinking about writing a book on blacksmithing, many things drifted across my mind. Some were enlightening and I have used them; others were clinkers, and I have put them in their proper place. These have been put in their place, the ash dump. Others persisted. These are my intuitive reactions to them:

Is blacksmithing an art, craft, trade or profession?

> Why worry about it? Call it anything you like, but make sure that you enjoy your work and develop your skills and artistry.

Should I be true to traditional blacksmithing and not use modern conveniences and tools?

> Why not? If you use them properly, they will save you time. Someone else had the good sense to invent them. You discover new ways to use them and create new forms with them.

I don't want to make a mistake, so I'm not going to try it!

> Sit on the riverbank and throw pebbles. This is easier than learning blacksmithing and you will never make a mistake. But, did you ever take a look at most smiths' scrap piles?

I can't write, so why write a book on blacksmithing, which I'm still learning?

> I got tired of throwing pebbles.

Index